HAUNTED DERBYSHIRE

AND THE PEAK DISTRICT

HAUNTED DERBYSHIRE
AND THE PEAK DISTRICT

*Wayne
Anthony*

The Breedon Books
Publishing Company
Derby

First published in Great Britain by
The Breedon Books Publishing Company Limited
Breedon House, 44 Friar Gate, Derby, DE1 1DA.
1997

ISBN 1 85983 087 0

Printed and bound by Butler & Tanner Ltd., Selwood Printing
Works, Caxton Road, Frome, Somerset.

Colour separations by RPS, Leicester.

Jackets printed by Lawrence-Allen, Weston-super-Mare, Avon.

Contents

Acknowledgements

I would like to thank the following people who have helped make this book possible: my wife Rachel for her patience; my sons Liam and Samuel for putting up with a grumpy father; Sir Geoffrey Rhadlon for the idea to write about ghosts in the first place; Clive Champion for helping me to obtain many of the pictures; Helen Meynell and Amanda Volley for their words of encouragement; the people of Derbyshire and the Peak District who have so kindly allowed me to intrude into their lives and who willingly gave me so much new information, never before recorded into the region's folklore; the staff at the *Derbyshire Now* magazine. The staff at the Local Studies Library in Derby, especially Lisa Bates who always seemed so willing to rummage through the archives to help, no matter how bizarre the request; Raymonds Photographers for allowing me to use some of their photographs; finally all my many other friends who have encouraged me.

Anyone wishing to add to this collection of ghost stories and curiosities is invited to write to me at 9 The Cottages, Hospital Lane, Mickleover, Derby DE3 5DR.

Wayne Anthony
Spring 1997

Introduction

by Wayne Anthony

DERBYSHIRE and the Peak District, two areas in part combined, are both regions which have undoubtedly managed to retain a magnificent array of remnants from an earlier age. Along with a well documented account of many of the legends and folklore of the region, there is also a large panoply of curiosities and peculiarities, magnificent houses, mansions, valleys and hills, all of which have their own curious stories to tell. The history of these places has helped to make these two areas of England, stand out just that little bit more than many other parts of the country.

Embroidered into that history is a rich tapestry of ghost stories, strange accounts, folklore, legends and some of the more curious aspects and features of nature. It is hoped that the reader will find a wide variety of some the more unusual aspects of our local history and perhaps some of these stories will enable us to take a slightly different look at our ancestry and age-old beliefs which we so often take for granted.

Although the majority of the Peak District lies within Derbyshire, a great deal of it also overlaps into Staffordshire while, north-west of Buxton, a significant area of the Peak District lies in Cheshire. The area has frequently been described as one of, if not the, most wealthy in ancient antiquities due partly to the fact that the terrain in which it lies is hilly and was at one time exceedingly inaccessible. The area was rich and self-sufficient and so dilution of the population did not occur at the same rate as elsewhere, emigration being virtually unnecessary whilst immigration was too small to actually make a big difference.

On the subject of ghosts and the paranormal, it is easy to dismiss that which we do not understand. What has the potential to change our opinions, which for the greater part have formed over many years, we often dismiss or ignore, choosing instead to retain that which is familiar and comfortable to our individual systems of belief. To many people the concept of ghosts is in itself frightening, and fear, as we know, often fixes our opinions. A philosopher once said, "Only to change is to find enlightenment," and perhaps there is great wisdom in these few simple words. Maybe we should allow ourselves to investigate such strange phenomena as ghosts and the supernatural, with open hearts as well as minds, suffering ourselves to change if we find the need and are presented with the relevant facts, yet also remembering that knowledge and understanding of the principles and workings of anything within this universe depends entirely on our flexibility to overcome fear.

However, this for many at the moment may be impossible to do, especially in a society which is content to dismiss anything that appears to be outdated or no longer needed. The stories that are to be found within the pages of this book are in no way necessarily my opinion. They are merely accounts of other people's experiences which have been presented so as to perhaps make us re-evaluate our stance on the paranormal. After all, can so many people with so many different ghost stories, and often with totally separate beliefs and cultural disciplines, be wrong?

Many scientists claim that ghosts are a trick of the light, or our over-tired minds casting images of reality in a way that makes us believe that we have seen something that is otherwise not there. While this may explain many of our ghostly encounters it in no way explains them all. For those of us who take a slightly more sceptical approach and who continually make statements that they have never personally experienced seeing a ghost – and until they do they will never believe in them – it is worth considering that these people have also never seen a thought wave, or the dark side of the moon, the centre of the earth, or love residing in the human heart, but we all know that these things do exist.

Many people ask me about my personal beliefs. I always feel this statement is a little sad, as surely what I believe is not particularly that important, surely what they believe is. We must simply adopt the philosophy with which we feel most comfortable. It would be wrong of me to try to convince anyone of anything. All I would recommend people to do is simply look at the facts, for there are many, then come to their own conclusion.

It is worth remembering that there are very few recorded incidents of ghosts harming anyone. Indeed, ghosts are perhaps more likely to be frightened of you, than you are of them. So, for now, let us look at some of the many types of ghosts we might encounter, more often than not, in the dark recesses of our own imaginations.

Haunted Halls and Houses

CHATSWORTH HOUSE

CHATSWORTH, how can I describe thee! Art thou not a gem of purest water dug out of the rugged mountains that surround thee, cut and bounded by a thousand facets with exquisite skill and admirable taste to set off thy native beauties? Surely thou art a very paradise, again established amongst the haunts of men again adorning our 'nether world!'

FOR CENTURIES people from all corners of the world have arrived in Derbyshire to admire and marvel at the beauty and splendour of Chatsworth House. People arrive in their thousands to admire this fabulous building, which has affectionately earned itself the title as 'The Palace of the Peak', and from earliest times gained the reputation of being one of the Seven Wonders of the Peak.

What we see of Chatsworth House today is in fact the work of many of the Cavendish family, whose fortunes were founded by the Countess of Shrewsbury, better known to us as Bess of Hardwick, who was originally a meagre daughter of an obscure Derbyshire farming squire. Many people consider Bess to have been obsessed with building houses but when we stop and consider what she achieved within her lifetime it is clear that apart from being a control freak she must also have been a remarkable lady for her foresight, determination and grit.

At the time of the Doomsday Book (AD1086), the area of Chatsworth was owned by Sir William Peveril of Peveril Castle, while the village of Edensor was in the possession of Henry de Ferrers who also owned Duffield Castle. Not a great deal is known of the early years of Chatsworth until 31st December 1549 when Sir William Cavendish, Bess of Hardwick's second husband, bought several properties, including Chatsworth for £600. It was three years after this date that Sir William Cavendish, no doubt encouraged by Bess, decided to build a house. The house was not quite finished when Sir William died on 25 October, 1557 and Bess mourned her loss deeply referring to him as 'my most deare and well beloved husband', other writings reveal that she often prayed to the lord 'to have Mercy and Ridd me and his poore Children out of our great Misserie', not that any of his children were ever 'Poore' as all of them became peers in their own right or married into the peerage.

Although after the death of Sir William Cavendish Bess was left with only a partly completed house and a great deal of debt, she relentlessly pushed on, and before long had married Sir William St Loe, who settled many of her debts, the remaining debts being wavered. The house was finally completed about 1560, and the cost is estimated to have finally been £80,000. Believed to have been grand for its time the original Chatsworth House comprised of a courtyard around which was built a four or five storey building with large square turrets at the corners. The main house faced the hillside as did the gardens, the reason being that the river was prone to flooding, so much so that seven small ponds were dug out near to the river, to catch excess water and hopefully hold it there. One of these ponds housed the Mary, Queen of Scots Bower which may still be seen today. Apart from the Mary, Queen of Scots Bower all that remains today of Bess' Chatsworth is the hilltop gazebo known affectionately as The Hunting Tower.

Bess of Hardwick's completed house, after all the time and toil it took to build, only managed to last a mere 150 years before being radically changed beyond its original state. Shortly after Bess married the 6th Earl of Shrewsbury, George Talbot, the house became a 'prison' for Mary, Queen of Scots, Bess and George found themselves playing host and captors of the unfortunate Queen. Mary who stayed at Chatsworth in the years 1570, 1573, 1577 and 1581 and it is believed that she may have stayed at the house on other occasions although there is little historical documentation to prove it.

In 1643 Chatsworth was garrisoned by forces under Sir John Gell, in the same year the Earl of Newcastle, having taken the manor of Wingfield, attacked and made himself master of Chatsworth House.

The third Earl of Chatsworth began to modernise the building internally in 1676, work also started on the gardens and were still continuing when the Earl died eight years later. Many of the internal alterations that the third Earl had made had left the structure of the house somewhat weakened. When the fourth Earl inherited the building in 1684, he deliberated on what to do about the poor state of the building and finally decided to pull the whole building down and start again. Not an easy decision to make, although I am sure one of the main influencing factors was the fact that the fourth Earl was disgraced from the royal court after he had led a certain Colonel Colepepper, out of the Presence Chamber, at Whitehall, for giving him an insulting look, once outside the Presence Chamber the Earl then struck him on the head with his cane. Later the Earl was summoned before the King's Bench, which found him guilty of assault, he was ordered to pay a £30,000 fine, refusing to do so the Earl retired to Chatsworth. The Earl never did pay the fine as the hurried abdication of King James in 1688, which Devonshire himself had helped force after meeting with Lord Delamare and the Earl of Danby, at the then Cock and Pynot Inn at Whittington

Moor, near Chesterfield, meant that the necessary fine papers were later destroyed. The fourth Earl was made the first Duke of Devonshire in 1694.

With his new title the first Duke of Devonshire decided to alter Chatsworth House some more and called in many leading craftsmen and artists of the day including Antonio Verrio and Louis Laguerre, who saw to much of the painted walls and ceilings. The gardens were also greatly altered with the cascade being added in 1694 and then enlarged again nearly a decade later when the cascade house was added.

Over the next five decades nothing much happened at Chatsworth until the fourth Duke, who unfortunately died young, decided on a single plan for the whole of the house and gardens, the river was straightened, the mill was removed and rebuilt at Beeley, the flood ponds were completely removed and the three arched bridge, which was designed and built by James Paine in 1761, at the front of the house, can still be seen today. All these changes, including the landscaping, were completed between the years 1755 and 1763. The fourth Duke greatly added to the wealth of Chatsworth in his marriage to the 16-year-old Charlotte Boyle. Through this marriage the Cavendishes obtained the Clifford estates of Bolton Abbey, the villa at Chiswick, Burlington House at Piccadilly and Londesborough in Yorkshire.

The fifth Duke did little to the splendour of Chatsworth House and is said to have been outwardly cold and somewhat lethargic although an intellect, he won the favour and finally the love of two of the most beautiful women of their time, Lady Elizabeth Foster and Lady Georgina Spencer, both of which he eventually married.

The sixth Duke ('the bachelor Duke') was a shy likeable gentleman who was slightly deaf and had a fondness for fine works of art, which he collected passionately. In 1818 he commenced work on Chatsworth by doubling its size when

Chatsworth House. Many ghosts haunt this magnificent house including a phantom grey lady, a white lady and a mysterious dark figure seen in the upper regions of the house.

he added the north wing in which the sculpture gallery, orangery, dining-room and theatre are located. It was the gardens however which received the most extensive attention after the Duke had employed Joseph Paxton at the age of 23 (later to achieve international fame for his designs at the great exhibition of 1851 and a knighthood), as his head gardener, after visiting the gardens of the Horticultural Society at Chiswick. Sir Joseph Paxton, as he later became, was as much a business man as he was a gardener, through his business sense and no doubt cautious nagging he managed to keep the estate's finances under control, despite the Duke's extravagant taste in art and finery. Within time Sir Joseph Paxton became the Duke's right-hand man and the Duke trusted his good opinion so much that he took him away with him to Europe. Within his time at Chatsworth he made many changes to the gardens his most famous work of art perhaps being the Emperor Fountain which he designed in 1843 to welcome Tsar Nicholas, Emperor of Russia, who was due to call in at Chatsworth on a visit to England. The Tsar never did make it to Chatsworth, his absence was said to have disappointed the Duke greatly as he had spent six months preparing the fountain which is capable of throwing a jet of water some 81 metres into the air and is fed by an eight acre lake, known as the Emperor Lake.

The seventh Duke undermined much of the great work done by Sir Joseph Paxton, although after Sir Joseph's death in 1865, the Duke wrote: 'There is no one whose personality will be more stamped on Chatsworth than Joseph Paxton's.'

The eighth Duke succeeded to the title at the age of 58 after a successful House of Commons career as Marquis of Hartington, a courtesy title carried by the Duke's heir. He was said to have been a typical aristocrat who had a slightly bumbling attitude and was widely known as being a bore. The ninth Duke was also a politician, albeit a frustrated one, and no doubt felt somewhat pressured having to take on Chatsworth House, after an uncle who was without an heir passed on. His 30-year stay at the house passed smoothly apart from a five-year stint as Governor-General of Canada. Within his time at the house he did some improvements with the help of architect W.H.Romaine-Walker, who greatly improved the Painted Hall. The Duke's heir succeeded him as tenth Duke in 1938 and was barely settled in when he was called away to war, the house then functioned as a refuge for the Penrhos College girls who were evacuated from Colwyn Bay.

Bess of Hardwick. Her ghost is reputed to haunt both Chatsworth House and Hardwick New Hall.

The present Duke (the 11th) and his wife, formerly Deborah Mitford, moved back to Chatsworth and have now restored the building to its former glory and through their business acumen have made Chatsworth House what it is today, a prosperous, magnificent building and fit for a King.

As to the ghosts that haunt Chatsworth house they are said to be many. Bess of Hardwick's ghost is believed to haunt the building and grounds. Having visited the building and talked with several of the guides it appeared obvious that they were somewhat reluctant to discuss the matter of ghosts, although several of them did inform me that the Duchess has seen several phantoms within the building throughout her stay there. Other stories came to light concerning a grey lady and a white lady seen wandering the corridors and rooms within the house. On several occasions footsteps have been heard,

doors have been seen to open and close by themselves and, according to one National Trust guide, the Duchess is said to have experienced this ghostly phenomena on several occasions within the library which houses one of the most extensive private collections of prints, books and old master drawings in the world. This opaque phantom is said to be seen gliding about the room, from shelf to shelf, as if looking for a particular book, or something else obscure we know not what.

Whilst touring the magnificent gardens I happened upon a young groundsman and asked him if he knew any stories concerning the alleged ghosts of Chatsworth House. To my great pleasure he told me several, mainly concerning the ghost of Mary, Queen of Scots (see Queen Mary's Bower), one story however concerned a workman who was making alterations to the building during World War Two. This gentleman was working in the upper regions of the house when he heard a great deal of commotion coming from somewhere about and below him. So loud were the noises that he found it almost impossible to concentrate on what he was doing, several times calling out to two people he believed were in the next room, for he could clearly hear the noise of muffled voices, again and again he shouted out to ask the other workmen to try and be a little more quiet. The noises however, banging, clattering, thumping etc., did not cease until shortly before he had finished the work at hand.

On leaving the building he met the then housekeeper who asked if everything had gone smoothly, "Yes" he grunted "apart from that there terrible racket them other workmen were making", looking at him bewildered the housekeeper informed him that there were no other workmen in the building and laughingly added that what he had heard must have been a ghost. The workman apparently went a deathly shade of white, gathered his tools and left the building as if the 'hounds of hell' were at his heels.

THE CHATSWORTH BRIDGE

THE ORNAMENTAL BRIDGE, which spans the River Derwent at Chatsworth House, has long had the reputation of being haunted. Each year a re-enactment of a tragic event, which took place many centuries ago, is said to replay itself on the bridge. The bridge itself is believed to have been designed by Caius Gabriel Cibber who carved many of the statues in the house and grounds, one legend had it that the bridge was designed by Michelangelo but we now know this was just romantic fantasy.

There are several versions to the story, the following appears to be the most popular. Two servants who once worked at the house fell in love and she inevitably fell pregnant. As the months passed the girl could conceal her secret no longer and left the house to live with some of her relatives at nearby Bubnell. Not long after the birth of her baby she was visited by the father of the child, (some versions of this story say that the father was a member of the aristocracy), who dragged the child from her arms and dashed out of the house towards the river, the screaming

Chatsworth Bridge. The ghost of a mother crying for her drowned child may be heard at certain times of the year.

mother in pursuit. On reaching the bridge near Chatsworth House the deranged man took the child in his arms and threw it into the cold dark swirling waters, needless to say the child drowned.

Other versions of the tale has it that the Earl of Devonshire, who just so happened to be passing by, rescued the child from its watery death, but, Stephen Glover in his *History of Derbyshire* recounts how: '1739. March 22. This evening the assizes ended, before Lord Chief Baron Page, when Mr James Loton, of Edensor, in the county of Derby, a man of good appearance and considerable substance, was tried and found guilty of the murder of a male bastard child, by drowning it, and received sentence of death, and to be hanged in chains. It appears from the subsequent papers, that great interest was made on his behalf to save his life. He was respited no less than six times, and finally, in the month of August, received a free pardon when he immediately went home to his family.'

A statue once stood on the bridge depicting this ancient tale, it was once toppled into the water to be rescued later, but alas it appears now to have gone forever. Walkers near the bridge may well hear the screams of the mother of the drowned child, who is said to haunt the bridge seeking to find her dead baby, other people of the district will tell you of the lonesome sad crying of a drowning baby which may still be heard on certain nights of the year.

BOLSOVER CASTLE

TODAY very little remains of the original Norman castle which was built in the 12th century by William Peveril. The building eventually fell into disrepair after it was besieged by King John in 1216. It was then demolished by Charles Cavendish in the early 17th century.

Numerous ghosts haunt the ruins of Bolsover Castle and are reported to appear on a regular basis. One lady visitor to the site had a terrifying experience when she visited the kitchens of the 'Little Castle'. No sooner had this lady walked into the kitchen than she was acutely aware of movement coming from an area of the kitchen where large baking ovens were situated. As she watched she saw to her horror a young woman come striding into the room carrying a bundle under her arm. The woman appeared to be frightened and looking apprehensive, she continuously glanced over her shoulder as if she was frightened and being pursued as she moved towards the ovens. The woman concerned watched the younger woman open the door to the ovens and shove the bundle she was carrying into the red hot coals which she could clearly see glowing within the oven. As the young woman did this the spectator suddenly became aware of a baby screaming, suddenly it dawned on her what was taking place and she moved towards the young woman, but, as she did so the images before her faded away into nothingness leaving only herself in the kitchens. She immediately left the building and told one of the custodians that she would never return to the castle again as she believed the castle to be an evil place.

Louis J.Jennings in *Rambles Among the Hills*, records how he was given a guided tour of the building by an elderly woman: 'We went downstairs, below the house itself, to the cellars and passages which are said to be the remains of the Norman structure. There was a high vaulted roof to the chamber now used as a kitchen, and an ancient stone passage connected it with a sort of crypt, beneath which, as the old woman said – and I can neither verify nor disprove her account,

Bolsover Castle. The ghost of a young woman placing a mysterious bundle into an oven within the kitchens of the 'Little Castle', has been seen here on several occasions.

but am content to take it as I received it – is a church, never opened since the days of William de Peveril, son of William the Conqueror. Our voices had a hollow sound; my footsteps awakened echoes from every corner. There must be some large empty space beneath the stone floor, but what it was used for in other days no one seems to know.

They say it has never been opened or examined. The chamber in which I stood was sufficiently strange – it might have been a wizard's cave, and all the world asleep. "This," I said in jest, "is where all your noises and ghosts come from." But the old woman answered very seriously, "It is, sir, and when the family are here the servants sometimes will not come down except by two or three. Oh, many people have seen things here besides me. Something bad has been done here, sir, and when they open that

church below, they'll find out. Just where you stand, by that door, I have several times seen a lady and gentleman – only for a moment or two, for they come like a flash. When I have been sitting in the kitchen, not thinking of any such thing, they stood there – the gentleman with ruffles on, the lady with a scarf around her waist. I never believed in ghosts but I have seen them. I am used to it now, and don't mind it. But we do not like the noises, because they disturb us. Not long ago, my husband who comes here at night, and I, could not sleep at all, and we thought at last that someone had got shut up in the castle, for some children had been here that day. So we lit a candle and went all over it, but there was nothing, only the noises following us, and keeping on worse than ever after we had left the rooms, though they stopped while we were in them".'

RIBER CASTLE

THIS folly was built in 1862 by John Smedley who was responsible for partly turning Matlock into a 19th-century spa town. After Smedley's death, Riber Castle functioned as a boys' school for just over a decade. During World War Two the building was used to store valuables and it was around this time that the castle began to fall into disrepair. Much has been done to the building over the last 20 years to enhance its structure.

Dracula's Castle, as it is often called, is said to be the haunt of two ghosts. The first is said to be a blue lady who is seen wandering the castle. The second ghost is reported to be a military type figure who marches through the walls of the castle.

Riber Castle – the haunt of a blue lady and a uniformed ghost.

BARLBOROUGH HALL

THE building of this beautiful hall, near the village of Barlborough, seven miles north-east of Chesterfield, has been accredited to Robert Smythson, the architect of Hardwick Hall, who built the house for Lord Justice Francis Rhodes in the 1580s. Francis was one of the judges who tried the ill-fated Mary, Queen of Scots. His carved stone figure, together with his wife, may be seen on a chimney piece within the house. The house is a characteristic example of the Elizabethan interpretation of Renaissance style, being square in plan, the house is perhaps more notable for its corner turrets, battlements and raised terrace.

Today the Hall functions as Mount St Mary's College, and has long had the reputation from its students of being haunted. The hall once had the fame of having housed a great long bow, this bow was said to have belonged to Robin Hood, legend makes the further claim that he was married to Maid Marion at a church nearby. For 200 years the ghost of a grey lady, occasionally reported to be blue has been said to be seen walking the halls and corridors of the building. Tradition tells of a groom being killed on his way

Barlborough Hall. A murdered priest, indelible bloodstains and a phantom coach and horses are all said to haunt the hall.

to be married at a nearby church. His bride to be, being the daughter of the house, hearing of his death, rushed back to Barlborough Hall and threw herself from the battlements, from that day onward she is said to be seen, when the moon is full, wandering the battlements looking for her lost love.

A room in the upper regions of the building is commonly known as the 'ghost room' having once been the scene of a murder in which a local recusant priest was killed whilst being concealed by the owners. His bloodstains are reputed to have remained on the floor of the room for many decades, occasionally they come back.

HARTINGTON HALL

ARTINGTON HALL which dates from 1350, (rebuilt in 1611), was the home of the Bateman family from the time that it was built until it was sold to the Youth Hostel Association. This is the same family as Thomas Bateman, the well known Derbyshire antiquary.

Robert Bateman, born in 1561, became a very successful merchant. One of his sons became knighted by King Charles II, whilst another became a Lord Mayor of London. The house boasts a 'Bonnie Prince Charlie Room' where the unsuccessful prince once stayed on his march to London in 1745.

The hall is said to be haunted by the ghost of a young woman who has been seen wandering from room to room in the early hours of the morning. One story concerning the ghost tells how a young lady, who once stayed at the youth hostel, awoke one night to find the wraith going

from bed to bed peering at who was sleeping in them. The lady awoke to find the ghost looking at her at which point she screamed and the ghost vanished.

Over the years several people who have stayed at the hall have experienced the same phenomena. The ghost is said to be looking for her lost love and, according to the legend, her lost love is no other than Bonnie Prince Charlie. Whilst he stayed at the hall he is purported to have fallen in love with a young maid who he apparently promised to return for once the political upheavals had died down. That day never came and the poor wretch is said to have lived the rest of her life at the hall as a spinster. Another version of the tale reiterates how she eventually died of a broken heart. From that day to this she wanders the house and occasionally the gardens, looking for the prince she thought loved her, perhaps hoping that one day he will return for her.

Hartington Hall, where the ghost of a servant awaits her prince.

FLAGG HALL

FLAGG HALL is a splendid example of an Elizabethan building which has for centuries concealed a secret that it shares with few — a skull which sits on a cheeseboard perched on a windowsill. The story of the Flagg Hall skull has been much overshadowed by the famous Dickey O'Tunstead. According to the legend the skull must remain at the hall as a totem of protection. If the macabre piece of ornamentation is removed then ill luck and strife will befall the property and its owners. The origin of the skull is unknown but like many other such skulls in the country it may well have come from a local burial mound, as it was once the fashion to collect and display unusual or grotesque artifacts. In

the 18th century William Burdekin lived at the hall. A relative of his recalls how she was once told that the skull was found at the hall and that they 'were going to re-bury it in Chelmorton churchyard. They all piled into the trap and set off, or rather they didn't, as the horse refused to move, no matter how it was coaxed or shouted at. So they all got down and went back into the house.'

On another occasion, after the skull had been reinstated in an attic room at the hall, a new servant was given the same room that the skull occupied. She took an instant dislike to the object and tossed it out of the window where it landed on a dung cart which was being taken to dump its load. The horse made such a fuss of kicking and jumping about that eventually the skull fell off the cart on to the road, where it was left lying for some time. Such ill luck befell the hall and its occupiers that they had to fetch the skull back, where it has remained until the present day, perched on a window sill on a staircase – no doubt the skull will continue to remain at the hall for some time yet.

SUDBURY HALL

THE Manor of Sudbury was recorded as being the property of Henry de Ferrers, of Duffield Castle, at the time of Domesday Book. The hall was built and lived in by the Vernon Family, a branch of the Haddon Hall Vernons. The estate was handed over to the National Trust in 1970.

There were three distinct phases of decoration at the hall. The first phase of decoration was completed by William Wilson and Samuel Mansfield. The second part was predominantly completed by Pettifer and Bradbury during the mid-1670s. In the 1690s, changing fashion dictated that the oval plaster-work on the ceilings should be enriched with extravagant mythical paintings. In 1691, the famous painter Louis Laguerre, was employed to repaint the ceilings with suitable subjects, this brought the decoration of the hall back in line with contemporary taste.

The Great Staircase is said to be haunted by William IV's widow, Queen Adelaide, who lived at the hall for several years. Her ghost is said to be seen to walk down the stairs dressed in black, looking sad and just before she reaches the bottom step she vanishes. A letter written by Queen Adelaide in 1841 requests, 'As private and as quick a funeral as possible with no procession and without pomp.' A facsimile of the whole letter can be seen at the hall.

Other ghosts are said to haunt the hall including a lady who, sporting a green velvet dress, is frequently seen wandering the upper rooms of the building. The ghost of a man who was drowned in the lake occasionally emerges from the dark waters covered in weed. The most curious ghost is that of a small-framed woman, who has been seen on numerous occasions wandering the grounds of the house. She is said to be dressed in a black shawl, wearing black boots with old fashioned buckles upon them, she is described as being no taller than 3ft high. Mrs Ford a former resident of Sudbury Village, describes seeing the phantom lady with her husband in January 1962 when: "As we passed Sudbury Hall, a wretched figure of an aged lady ran out in front of our car and my husband had to brake suddenly to avoid running over her. I watched her reach the other side of the road, at which point she vanished, leaving no trace of her ever having been there. If my husband and I had not seen it with our own eyes, we would never have believed it."

Many other rooms at the hall are

Sudbury Hall. Numerous ghosts are said to haunt the hall and grounds.

also believed to be haunted, especially the boiler room where several members of staff have been unable to open the door once inside. One member of staff described how he once tried to open the cellar door to get down to the boiler room. "The door is never locked but it wouldn't budge. I had to get a crowbar but it still wouldn't move. Then as if by magic it sprung open on its own." The gentleman concerned continues: "On another occasion a workman was in the boiler room up a ladder at near ceiling height when he felt a tap on his shoulder. He turned expecting to see a colleague but nobody was there. He was so scared he refused to work down there again."

Other ghostly happenings have occurred at the hall including a previous worker who awoke one night to find the ghost of a maid watching over her baby daughter. Another bedroom is the haunt of a small girl who was burnt to death there in a tragic accident.

ERRWOOD HALL

LOCATED within the Peak District National Park is the beautiful Goyt Valley, which in turn harbours the ruins of Errwood Hall, built in 1830 by Samuel Grimshaw. The building was constructed in Italian style and the family are said to have lavishly entertained guests and friends. The estate totalled 496 acres and gave work to a host of gardeners, servants, gamekeepers and a private school. The hall was once used as a youth

Errwood Hall. Several ghosts haunt the ruins of this hall, including a previous owner and a former tutor to the Grimshaw family children.

hostel before finally being demolished in 1934 to make way for the two reservoirs, Fernilee Reservoir built in 1938 and later Errwood Reservoir built in 1967. All that remains today is a row of windows to the south front and a small family cemetery located within the gardens. In the 19th century the Grimshaw family planted over 40,000 rhododendrons, which may still be seen today.

The area is a popular tourist attraction especially when all the flowers are in bloom.

Numerous ghosts are said to haunt the old ruins of the hall, a former servant, several dogs and a one-time female tutor to the Grimshaw children. The Governess is frequently seen roaming the remains of the hall and the gardens. She appears dressed in a long flowing dress and sporting a large-brimmed hat, she wanders about and has been known to smile and greet people visiting the site. The ghost is also known to haunt the small cemetery near the hall where she has been seen looking at the grave stones with a sad look upon her face.

Another ghost which haunts the area is that of Mary Gosselin who died in 1930 and was buried in the family cemetery. It is said that her death was hastened by the news that the council were going to demolish the hall to make way for a reservoir. Her ghost is seen wandering the gardens, especially in late autumn.

RENISHAW HALL

SITUATED midway between Eckington and Renishaw, the hall is the home of the Sitwell family. Built in 1625 the hall has changed very little over the last 300 years.

In 1885 a party of distinguished guests were visiting Sir George Sitwell at the hall. Amongst the visitors was Dr Tait, the then Archbishop of Canterbury, and his daughter. After the guests had retired to bed and a hush had fallen over the house, Miss Tait awoke in middle of the night by what she later described as three cold kisses. So disturbed by the experience Miss Tait took up refuge in an adjacent bedroom which was occupied by Sir George's daughter. Miss Sitwell confessed that she too had had a very similar experience when sleeping in that particular room. Subsequent discussion and investigation revealed that other members and guests of the household had also suffered the same cold phantom kisses when sleeping in that particular room.

Some time after this occurrence the house suffered some minor alterations. The haunted room and the room beneath it were demolished to make way for a larger staircase. While the work was being carried out a strange and macabre discovery was made. During the removal of the floor of the haunted room an empty coffin was found which had been fastened to the joists of the floor with iron clamps. Further investigations of the coffin revealed that it was probably made in the 17th century and from marks found on and in the coffin it was decided that at one time it undoubtedly would have held a corpse.

Further ghostly occurrences, as far as we know, were absent from the hall until 1909, when Sir George Sitwell wrote to Lord Halifax, a famous ghost hunter and writer of numerous books, to report further ghostly happenings at the hall: 'Last Saturday two ghosts were seen at Renishaw. Lady Ida had been to Scarborough to attend the Life Boat Ball, at which she had sat till four o'clock in the morning, returning home in the afternoon. After dinner, the party of six – I was absent for a few hours – sat in the drawing room upstairs, Lady Ida lying on the sofa facing the open door. She had been speaking to a friend who was sitting on her left when she looked up and saw in the passage outside the figure of a woman, apparently a servant, with grey hair and a white cap, the upper part of her dress being blue and her dress dark. Her arms were stretched out at full length and the hands were clasped. The figure moved with a very slow, furtive, gliding motion as if wishing to escape notice, straight towards the head of the old staircase, which I removed 20 years ago. On reaching it she disappeared. Unwilling to think that there was anything supernatural in the appearance, Lady Ida called out, "Who's that?" and then the name of the housekeeper. When no one answered she cried to those nearest the door, "Run out and see who it is: run out at once."

The letter goes on to describe how a thorough search of the house was made which revealed no one. On returning from the search an accomplice claimed that they had seen the ghost of a woman standing outside a door which once led to where the ghost room had been before the staircase had been put in.

'Two people rushed out, but no one was to be seen, nor, when the others joined them and searched the hall and passage upstairs, could they find anyone resembling the woman described to them by Lady Ida. They had given up the search and were returning to the drawing room, when one of the party, Miss★★★R, who was a little behind the others, exclaimed, "I do believe that's the ghost!" No one else saw anything, but after-wards she described what she had seen. In the full light of the archway below, within 20ft of her, and just where the door of the old ghost room used to stand, until I removed it and put the present staircase in its place, she saw the figure of a lady with dark hair and dress, apparently lost in painful thought and oblivious to everything about her. Her dress was fuller than is the modern fashion and the figure though opaque, cast no shadow. It moved with a curious gliding motion into the darkness and melted away at the spot within a yard of the place where a doorway, now walled up, led from the staircase to the hall.

"There is no doubt that these figures were actually seen as described. They were not ghosts but phantasms, reversed impressions of something seen in the past, and now projected from an over tired and excited brain. In both cases the curious gliding motion, the absence of shadow and the absolute stillness of the figures, which moved neither hand nor head and hardly seemed to breath, point to that conclusion. Such an experience goes far towards solving the ghost problem."

Lady Ida later added further note which stated that she 'saw the figure with such distinctness that I had no doubt at all that I was looking at a real person. I was conscious of an uneasy, creepy feeling. The figure was that of a woman between 50 and 60 years of age her grey hair was done up into a 'bun', under an old fashioned cap.'

MELBOURNE HALL

AT the time of the Domesday Book the area of Melbourne belonged to the Royal Manor, King John came here on at least five separate occasions. In the 15th century a castle existed at Melbourne, and John of Bourbon, the most important prisoner to be taken at the Battle of Agincourt in 1415, was detained here for nearly two decades. Legend has it that Mary, Queen of Scots was also held prisoner at the castle. In the 17th century the castle at Melbourne was allowed to fall into disrepair, today all that remains of the castle is a wall. On the south side of the hall is Melbourne Pool, the waters of which are said to cover a quarry from which, according to legend, the

Melbourne Hall, the haunt of two white ladies.

stone for the castle was extracted. Through the Middle Ages the Manor of Melbourne was part of the enormous estates of the Duchy of Lancashire.

In 1133, Henry I founded the Bishopric of Carlisle, one of its very first endowments was Melbourne Church. Carlisle, being so close to the borders of England and Scotland, made it a prime target for raids by the Scots. Being tired of continuously being harassed, the Bishops of Carlisle retired to Derbyshire when trouble threatened, this is primarily one of the reasons why they built the magnificent church that we see at Melbourne today. The church was built between 1133 and 1229, the large size of the church is due to the bishops needing to still carry out there duties when Carlisle was being raided. In 1299, Henry III granted Melbourne to Walter Mauderc, the Bishop of Carlisle at that time. Later he built a palace, and eventually managed to obtain permission to hold ordinations at the church, the Bishops of Carlisle were at residence at Melbourne for nearly 500 years.

The hall was leased from the Bishops of Carlisle by Sir John Coke in 1628, Secretary of State to Charles I, who converted the building for use as his own home, using the stones from the old Melbourne castle, he was the founding father of the Melbourne Hall we see today. Sir John's great-grandson, Sir Thomas Coke, who lived at the hall from 1696, altered the house giving it the east façade, and before that the gardens which are still among the finest of their style remaining in England. Sir Thomas sought the advise of two of the foremost garden land-

scape designers of the time, George London and Henry Wise, who replanned and enlarged the gardens. One of the most interesting features of the garden, and perhaps its most famous, is the unique arbour, known locally as the 'Birdcage' which was designed and built by Robert Bakewell, (1682-1752), Derby's most famous ironsmith. Other works by Robert Bakewell include the font cover in St Werburgh's Church Derby, the Cathedral gates, Foremark Church altar rails, Longford Hall gates and the screen at Staunton Harold Church.

Sir Thomas Coke had no son from either of his marriages so his youngest daughter Charlotte, inherited Melbourne Hall and through her marriage to Matthew Lamb, the house passed to a different family line. Charlotte's husband, Matthew Lamb, who came from a humble beginning, was said to have been an ambitious man who, at the time of his death, was worth over a million pounds. Later Matthew gained a seat in the Commons and later a baronetcy. His son, Sir Peniston Lamb, was created a peer in 1780 and was known as Viscount Melbourne. His second son, William, born 1779, eventually inherited the title and later became Queen Victoria's first Prime Minister.

William, 2nd Viscount Melbourne, was once described by Lord David Cecil as 'a cynic who

The Bird Cage. The tragic figure of Caroline Ponsonby is reputed to haunt both the wrought-iron summer house and the yew tree arbour.

loved mankind, a sceptic who found life thoroughly worth living', and 'a happy man on the whole'. When he was 21 he met and fell in love with 14-year-old Caroline Ponsonby. Four years after the two had met, they married, and for three years led a very happy life. Caroline was very beautiful but was known to suffer from mental illness. She is rumoured to have had several affairs whilst still married to William, notably Lord Byron, Caroline later went completely insane and eventually died in 1828. She bore William one child, a boy, which they named Augustus, who was retarded from birth, he died in early manhood.

William never married again although his name appeared as correspondent in two divorce cases, both of which went in his favour. When he died the viscountancy went to his childless brother where upon his death the title became extinct. After his death the Melbourne Estate passed to his sister, Emily Lamb, who was married to the 5th Lord Cowper. The hall stayed in the Cowper family for the next 40 years, until Lady Annabel Cowper married Lord Walter Kerr, Admiral of the Fleet. In 1906 Lord and Lady Kerr made Melbourne Hall their home, Peter, their grandson, became the 12th Marquis of Lothian after the death of his cousin in Washington in 1940. The present owner is the Marquess of Lothian, Chief of Clan Kerr, who still maintains the quality and beauty of a house and gardens which has been described by several writers as being 'one of the most beautiful in the country'.

Two ghosts are said to haunt the hall, both are 'white Ladies'. The first ghost is said to be seen wandering between the house and the church of St Martin's. She is described as young, perhaps in her 20s, wearing long flowing garments. This ghost has also been spotted inside the church, and on several occasions has been noted standing not too far from the altar. Near to the altar is the capitals, upon which is a carved a grotesque figure of a Shiela-na-Gig, an ancient representation of a pagan mother earth fertility goddess.

The second ghost is said to be that of the tragic Caroline Ponsonby, her ghost is seen wandering the area around the 'Birdcage', having first appeared from the hall, her sylph-like figure sweeps across the neatly laid out lawns and borders, then passing across, or close by the square pool she vanishes into the arbour. When I visited the hall, a local gentleman, who was familiar with the ghost story, informed me that at one time Caroline's ghost haunted several stone steps near the square pool, so frequent were her appearances that eventually the gardeners at the hall were

*The Dark Arbour at
Melbourne Hall.*

instructed to remove them in the hope that this would lay the ghost. Apparently it worked and she now haunts the arbour. Another version of this story concerns the steps being washed away in a flood, at which point Caroline's ghost moved itself to the area she haunts today. Her ghost is also alleged to haunt a spectacular 100 yard long Yew Tunnel, which is believed to have been planted in the time of Charles I.

HAZLEBADGE HALL

THE HALL WAS built in 1549 and was part of a dowry when Dorothy Vernon married Sir John Manners in the 16th century. Today the building functions as a farmhouse, a coat of arms bearing the Vernon crest dated 1549 can be seen above a mullioned window that faces a road which skirts the farm.

The 300-year-old ghost story associated with the hall, appears to have first been published in the latter part of the 19th century and is as follows:

'On any wild night, when the winds howl furiously and the rain falls in torrents, there can be seen in the gorge between Bradwell and Hazlebadge, the spirit of a lady on horseback, the steed rushing madly in the direction of the old hall. It is said to be the ghost of Margaret Vernon, the last of that line of the Vernons who were living at Hazlebadge for three centuries. She had given her heart, with its fullness of affection, unto the keeping of one who had plighted his troth with another, and when she had discovered his treachery she had braced up her nerves to witness his union in Hope Church. But at the finish of the ceremony she had ridden to her home as if pursued by fiends, with eyeballs starting from their sockets, and her brain seized with a fever from which she would never have recovered only from the tender nursing of those around her. Her spirit, they say, on a spectre steed, is still seen rushing between Hope and Hazlebadge at midnight.

HADDON HALL

THE DOMESDAY BOOK in 1086 records the owner of the hall as Henry de Ferrers. Later the house was to be granted to William Peveril, but after the poisoning of the Earl of Chester, King Henry II confiscated all the lands of the de Ferrers. The tenants of the property at that time was the Avenell family, they continued to occupy the hall for another 40 years. About 1190 Richard de Vernon married Alice Avenell, co-heiress to William de Avenell, Lord of Haddon. As a result of this union the hall eventually passed into the hands of the Vernon family, there it would stay for the next 350 years.

The hall once again changed hands into the Manners family, via Dorothy Vernon, in 1567, when she married Sir John Manners, second son of Thomas Manners, the Earl of Rutland. The hall has remained in the Manners family ever since.

The most famous story concerning Haddon Hall is surely that of Dorothy Vernon and Sir John Manners. Tradition tells how Dorothy's father, Sir George, forbade her to have anything to do with Sir John. According to the legend, of which there are several versions, conflict lay in their differing religious beliefs, Dorothy's family were Protestants and John's Catholics, other versions of the tale state that Dorothy had been betrothed to another influential gentleman.

Having fallen in love with John, Dorothy attempted at every given opportunity to be with him. Sir George forbade her to have anything to do with John and posted a servant to watch her by night and day. Her stepmother, and sister Mar-

Dorothy Vernon's Steps. Her ghost is still seen running down these steps.

Dorothy Vernon's tomb at Bakewell Church.

garet, also kept a wary eye on Dorothy's movements, reporting back to Sir George all her activities, Dorothy was virtually kept a prisoner at the hall. On the night of her sister's wedding, when all the guests and her family were merrily occupied with the festivities, Dorothy slipped away. She is said to have left via the steps off the long gallery and met John Manners, who had disguised himself as a woodsman, on the packhorse bridge, which may still be seen today.

Together the young couple eloped to Leicestershire where they were married the very next day at Aylestone. Later Sir George became reconciled to the marriage, and on his death in 1567 Dorothy inherited the Derbyshire estates.

Dorothy died in 1584, John Manners outlived her by 27 years and never re-married. John, who is said to have loved Dorothy with all his heart, created a wonderful tomb for her body to lie in, their effigies appearing together in alabaster can still be seen at Bakewell church.

Dorothy's ghost is said to haunt the Hall, and her gossamer white spirit can be seen running down the steps just off the long

Haddon Hall. Said to be the most romantic house in Derbyshire.

gallery, looking back as if someone were chasing her. The steps are known as the 'Dorothy Vernon Steps', her ghost has also been seen in other areas of the house and garden. Haddon Hall is also the haunt of a monk, a blue lady, seen in the long gallery and a little boy. Strange things often happen at the Hall, according to one groundsman, footsteps are frequently heard in many parts of the house without any visible sign of any person being there. Phantom music has also been heard emanating from the old Vernon Chapel.

HARDWICK HALL

'Higher yet in the very east frontier of this county, upon a rough and craggie soile standeth Hardwic, which gave name to a family in which possessed the same: out of which descended Lady Elizabeth, Countess of Shrewsbury, who beg-anne to build there two goodly houses joining in a manner one to the other, which by reason of their lofty situation shew themselves, a farre off to be seene, and yeeld a very goodly prospect.'
William Camden, Britannia, 1610.

THE STONE initials E.S that crown this magnificent hall proclaims its builder – Bess of Hardwick – Matriarch of many Derbyshire gentry and builder of houses. Born at Hardwick in 1518, one of a

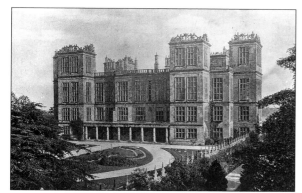

Hardwick New Hall. The ghost of Elizabeth Shrewsbury still haunts this place.

family of four girls and one boy, Elizabeth's father, a small landowner whose family had been established at Hardwick for at least six generations, died in 1528, leaving each of his daughters £26 13s 4d.

Soon after her father's death Bess went to live with Sir John and Lady Zouche at one of their houses. There she met and later married her cousin Robert Barlow, heir to a Derbyshire family, who were slightly more prosperous than her own. When she was barely 14 years of age Robert Barlow died 'before they were bedded', according to one report. This was the pattern of things to come, for in her lifetime Bess was to be married four times, and each time she inherited a fortune.

In 1547, Bess married Sir William Cavendish, at 2am in the Grey Family Chapel at Bradgate Manor Leicestershire. The second marriage produced eight children of which six lived, three boys and three girls. William Cavendish was an extremely wealthy government servant who, although getting on in years, was still a handsome man. To please his new wife William sold most of his properties, of which there were many, then purchased new property and land in Derbyshire and Nottinghamshire. Amongst the new properties that were purchased was the house and estate of Chatsworth, which he bought in 1549. A new house was built on the site of the Chats-

worth House that we see today. In 1557 William Cavendish died, leaving Bess most of his wealth. Two years later she was married again, this time to a wealthy West Country landowner, Sir William St Loe. This marriage was yet another step up for Bess for, apart from being wealthy and a Captain of the Guard, William St Loe was also a favourite of Queen Elizabeth I. This marriage only managed to last five years, Sir William died in 1565, leaving the majority of his wealth to Bess, much to the disgust and anger of several members of his family.

Her fourth marriage in 1567, about which there had been much speculation, was to George Talbot 6th Earl of Shrewsbury, a widower with six children. At the age of 40, George Talbot was a wealthy man, a landowner, a merchant of coal and glass, amongst other things, and belonged to one of the richest families in England. Shortly after this union there was a double marriage in the parish church of Sheffield, George's second son Gilbert married Bess' daughter Mary, and his youngest daughter Lady Grace Gilbert, married Bess' eldest son Henry, thus strengthening the families position even more.

After two years of living in relative happiness, George Talbot was given custody of Mary, Queen of Scots, just after she had fled across the English border in 1569. He remained her captor until 1584, within that time Mary was constantly moved between his many houses, Sheffield Castle, Tutbury Castle, Wingfield Manor, Chatsworth House, Worksop Manor and his lodge at Buxton.

Legend has it that she stayed at Hardwick Hall, however, many historians dispute this claim stating that there is no real evidence of her ever having stayed there, the building of the hall having started three years after she was executed, even though a coat of arms, similar to her own, now in the British Museum, can be seen above a chamber in the house known as the Mary, Queen of Scots Room. The panelling for this

Hardwick Old Hall. The famous Thomas Hobbes, philosopher and tutor, died at the hall in 1679. His ghost may still be seen walking the pathway beneath the old house.

room was probably moved there from Chatsworth House.

Having custody of Mary, Queen of Scots proved to be too much pressure for the couple, putting the marriage under an enormous amount of strain, even Queen Elizabeth I, and her Privy Council, could do little to ease the situation. In 1583 rumours began to circulate, probably spread by Bess and her son, that George Talbot was having an affair with the captive Queen. This appeared to be the final straw, and very shortly after these rumours the marriage collapsed completely.

During the collapse of their marriage much bickering between the two took place, Bess insisted that she wanted Chatsworth House, George insisted that she could not, neither was prepared to give it up. Eventually George attempted to take the house by force, and even though the Queen's Privy Council had instructed him to let her have one of his properties he refused, making life for Bess as difficult as possible.

Bess, realising that she was getting nowhere arguing with George, purchased Hardwick from her brother James, who had built up a great deal

of debt over several years. Once Hardwick was in her possession she immediately began to build, between 1585 and 1590, Bess replaced the old house with what we now call Hardwick Old Hall.

In 1590 Lord Shrewsbury died. His final years were spent, some say miserably, living with a mistress in a house near Sheffield. Bess, by this time in her early seventies, was now one of the richest women in England. Rather than move into Chatsworth House, perhaps because of the unhappy memories, she decided to start building yet another house, the plans were drawn up and commencement of the property, which was only a few hundred yards away from the still unfinished Hardwick Old Hall, got underway.

The new hall, built with stone quarried from the base of the hill it stands on, was constructed in the shape of an H, and designed by Robert Smythson, whose family have been involved in many of Derbyshire's finest houses such as Bolsover Castle and Barlborough Hall. Bess lived for ten years in her new hall, and finally died there in 1608 on 13th February, at the age of 90. Bess was buried in great state at the church of All Hallows, Derby, now the cathedral. Her tomb is perhaps one of the grandest, even if it is slightly pretentious, in Derbyshire.

Edmund Lodge in his book *'Illustrations of British History'* 1791, describes Bess in a much quoted passage as: 'A woman of masculine understanding and conduct, proud, furious, selfish and unfeeling, she was a builder, a buyer and seller of estates, a moneylender, a farmer and a merchant of lead, coals and timber when disengaged from these employments she intrigued alternately with Elizabeth and Mary, always to the prejudice and terror of her husband.'

No other Elizabethan house like Hardwick has survived with as many original contents, as listed in an inventory dated 1601. Although the hall contains world-famous Elizabethan furniture, paintings and tapestries, it is better known for its impressive embroideries which date from the late 16th and early 17th centuries, all are thought to have been made especially for, or at the hall. The survival of many the embroideries owes much to Evelyn, Duchess of Devonshire, whose husband, the 9th Duke inherited the house in 1908. Over the next 50 years of her residence at the hall, Evelyn took it upon herself to ensure that many of the tapestries and embroideries were restored and repaired.

When visiting the hall I was informed by several of the custodians that the house was haunted by numerous ghosts. The most frequently sighted ghost of recent years is that of a white-faced monk seen wandering the grounds. Several writers have written about this ghost although, according to one of the custodians at the hall, the ghost was no more than a local gentleman who took great pleasure dressing up as the monk and wandering the countryside half frightening people to death. Later he would meet with friends in a local public house and laugh and joke at how many tourists he had managed to scare that day. That there are real ghosts at Hardwick Hall however is indisputable, too many people have seen too many strange

things. Both halls are reputed to be the haunts of a phantom blue lady, who has been seen dozens of times, often wandering the perimeter wall of the old hall. A ghostly white cat is frequently seen wandering the house and gardens, and there have been many reports of people seeing the animal vanish before their eyes. The ghost cat is said to especially favour haunting the Needlework Room and the chapel landing.

Men working on the building frequently report strange happenings including moans, banging and crashing sounds, footsteps behind them and whispering noises coming from the adjacent room in which they were working. The property manager Christopher Corry-Thomas reiterated to me several stories concerning the ghosts at Hardwick, he however had never seen anything unusual and although he did not believe any of the stories he did not disbelieve them either.

The Blue Bedroom, situated within the new hall is, according to one lady custodian 'The centre of all, the hauntings,' visitors to the hall frequently report the sensation of being watched whilst in there. Many people agree that there is a definite presence within the room, which is often icy cold, whilst others claim to have been touched or spoken to by an invisible personality. This lady went on to tell me that on numerous occasions the beds within the upper rooms of the building were frequently found to have indentations upon them, as if some unseen individual had been lying upon them.

A previous housekeeper once experienced the ghost when she was working in an apartment within the house known as the Flower Room. The housekeeper was busily ironing and folding clothes when she was distracted, from her work by an assistant in the corridor outside the room in which she was working. She chatted to the other assistant, who wanted directions on a job she was working on, for no more than a minute. On returning to her task she discovered that the ironing, which she had so painstakingly worked

Thomas Hobbes the philosopher. His ghost is said to walk the outer wall of the garden at the old Hardwick Hall.

upon, now all lay crumpled up in a heap.

Two famous ghosts that haunt the hall are Thomas Hobbes, philosopher and author of *Leviathan* and *Behemoth,* and Mary, Queen of Scots. Although it has previously been stated that there is no evidence to show that Mary ever stayed at the property, a ghost of a blue lady, seen in the Long Gallery, is said by many to be her. Thomas Hobbes, who became tutor to the 3rd Earl, and remained his patron and protector for the rest of his life, stayed at the hall for many years. At the end of his long career he retired to Chatsworth and Hardwick. At Hardwick he was known to walk up and down the hill 'till he was in a great sweat then give the servants some money to rub him'. He believed that these practises would make him healthier and enable him to live longer. Thomas Hobbes died at Hardwick in 1679 aged 91, and was buried at the parish church at Ault Hucknall. His ghost is still said to wander the grounds of the house, especially the path that runs beneath the walls of the old hall.

KEDLESTON HALL

Grant me ye gods a pleasant seat
In attick elegance made neat
Fine lawns, much wood, and
   water plenty
(of deer, & herds, & flocks not
   scanty)
Laid out in such an uncurb'd taste
That nature mayn't be lost but
   grac'd

Sir Nathaniel Curzon, 1st Lord Scarsdale

KEDLESTON HALL is one of the greatest designs of Robert Adam who was responsible for much of the success of the Neo-classical movement in Great Britain. The house is designed in a Greek and Roman fashion, a trend which was held by many of the English landowners in the 18th century.

Sir Nathaniel Curzon, who later became the 1st Lord Scarsdale, enlisted the help of some of the more traditional architects. In 1758, after Robert Adam had returned from studying in Rome, he was given full charge of building the house.

The main block was never intended to be lived in, its function was purely to entertain friends and to show off the numerous works of art and sculptures – most of which can still be seen today. The family resided in one of the two flanking side pavilions, the other pavilion contained kitchens and quarters for the workers at the hall. Two other pavilions were originally designed for the house but these were never built.

The old village and public highway, which originally existed near the house, were moved, under the instruction of Lord Scarsdale, beyond

Kedleston Hall. Heavy breathing, banging doors and mysterious phantom footsteps have all been experienced at the hall.

the boundaries of the present park during the construction of the new house. The formal gardens were swept away and new ponds and lakes were built giving the gardens a less austere look. Many of the other buildings within the gardens, including the fishing pavilion, the bridge and the cascade, were designed by Robert Adam.

In the 20th century the treasures of the house were further enriched with a collection of Eastern treasures gathered by the Marquis Curzon, who collected the treasures whilst he was the Viceroy of India.

A house has existed at Kedleston since Medieval times. In 1066, the owner of Kedleston was Earl Godwin, the father of Harold II, the last of our Saxon Kings. Two decades later the manor was held by Gilbertus, a tenant and friend of Henry de Ferrers of Duffield Castle. From 1100 to 1135, the tenant is recorded as being Richard de Curzon, son of Giraline de Curzon – companion of arms to William the Conqueror. The next tenant was Robert de Curzon, whose wife bore him two sons, Thomas and Richard.

Thomas married a girl called Sybil, she too had a son and also called him Thomas. He was brought up by his uncle, Richard, as his own father died whist he was still young. In 1198 the inheritance was divided between the two of them, Richard inherited the Croxall estate, whilst Thomas inherited the Kedleston Manor, village and church. From Thomas came a completely unbroken bloodline of male heirs which was to last until the present day.

The Church, dedicated to All Saints, is all that remains of the original village of Kedleston. Within this church are buried many generations of the Curzon family. Perhaps the grandest of all the monuments in the church is that which was erected in 1906, by Lord Curzon Viceroy of India and Foreign Secretary. The monument, erected in memory of Mary Leiter, the daughter of a Chicago millionaire, depicts the two in a recumbent position. Carved in purest Serravezza marble by Sir Bertram Mackennal, the Viceroy is shown wearing his robes of the Knight Grand Cross of the Order of the Star of India.

In a side passage leading to what was the stable

Thomas Chatterton. This marble figure of a disgraced poet, who took his own life, haunts the grounds of the hall.

found no more work as a writer, he was excommunicated from the literary scene, and the poet was eventually reduced to handing out pamphlets and begging for scraps of food from friends, who eventually all turned their backs on him.

The final morbid twist to this tale came when Chatterton, by now desperate, starving, depressed, and denied credit by everyone he knew, went to a chemist and complained that his flat was infested with rats – the pharmacist dispensed arsenic. On 24th August 1770, the tragic Chatterton committed suicide by swallowing arsenic, aged just 17.

The recumbent marble figure of Chatterton, placed at the hall by Lady Otterly, who, being familiar with the tragic story, took a shine to the statue and brought it back to the house where it still remains today.

Of the many ghosts that are said to haunt the hall, Chatterton's is said to be the most frequently seen. He is said to appear on moonlit nights, and is seen wandering the gardens. One lady worker at the hall informed me that on two occasions she had seen the ghost of Chatterton, once when she was leaving the hall late one evening, and again on a foggy day from an upstairs window, where she watched the pale ghostly and 'unhappy looking figure' walking in the gardens.

Other workers at the hall have experienced strange phenomena including, being spoken to by an unseen presence, footsteps being heard in the upper regions of the house, doors banging and the sound of someone breathing very heavily in the Saloon, when no one but the custodian, was in there.

yards, lies a tragic marble figure of a man who lusted after fame and fortune and was denied both. In 1768 Thomas Chatterton perpetuated a major fraud by producing a group of poems, said to have been written by a 15th-century monk named Thomas Rowley. The poems were well received by the people of the time and Chatterton enjoyed a great deal of success until his hoax came to light. His victims, furious at being cheated, extracted their revenge. People in power at the time made sure that this young man

SUTTON SCARSDALE HALL

NOW a forlorn ruin, this once great mansion, located on the opposite side of the valley from Hardwick Hall, was at one time described as being one of the most magnificent houses in Derbyshire. The hall was once the home of the Arkwright family, but was originally built in 1780, by the fourth Earl of Scarsdale. A much older building occupied the site before the present one was built.

Sutton Scarsdale Hall. It is here that a disembodied ghostly arm beckons you into the bowels of the building.

One of the ancient owners of the hall feature in a well-known Derbyshire legend concerning the Crusades. Sir Nicholas Leake was a noble knight who, believing it was his duty to fight in the Crusades, one day decided to set of immediately for the Holy Land. Before he left he drew his wife to him and kissing her passionately vowed to return to her as soon as possible. Before he left he took from his finger their wedding band and cleaving it in two with his sword offered the second half to his wife as a pledge of his fidelity.

During a battle with the Turks Sir Nicholas was taken prisoner and held by the Turks for ransom. Several years passed and the knight became very weary and dishevelled by his long imprisonment. Deciding one night to pray, he knelt in the small room in which he was confined and prayed fervently to God, vowing that if ever he managed to be restored to his wife in England he would make ample provisions for the poor of his parish. And then he fell asleep. When he awoke he miraculously found himself in the porch of the parish church of Sutton and immediately took himself back to the hall. The years of imprisonment had taken their toll on Sir Nicholas and his features were barely recognisable. On arriving at the hall he presented himself to his servants who mistook him for some impostor who was trying to impersonate their master in order to obtain possession of the hall and its treasures. An audience with his wife was repeatedly refused and he was driven away from the hall with the threat that if he returned they would have him imprisoned. Wandering away from the hall he had not travelled far before he suddenly remembered the broken ring which he had kept all these years hidden on his person. Once again he bravely returned to the hall, where he pleaded with the servants to take the broken half of the ring to his wife. This they eventually agreed to do, and on seeing the other half of the ring, which matched perfectly to the one his wife had kept. Sir Nicholas' wife ran to him and there followed a joyous reunion and many years of happiness.

True to his promise to God for his miraculous deliverance Sir Nicholas Leake made provisions in his will for seven bushels of wheat to be baked into loaves and given to the poor of Sutton, Temple Normanton and Duckmanton on each St Nicholas Day. This custom was still maintained until the death of Nicholas Leake, the last Earl of Scarsdale in 1736.

Today the hall is a sad reminder of how a property should not be treated. The ghosts that haunt the hall are believed to be numerous and include the phantom fragrance of tobacco which is smelt in several parts of the building, lights of a mixed hue, which appear then hover for several seconds before vanishing and a disembodied arm that beckons the observer towards the cellar area of the building.

It has been suggested by one former gentleman who worked as a labourer at the ruin, that some nefarious deed once took place down in the bowels of the building. Another ghost manifests itself in the sound of phantom footsteps which are frequently heard wandering the building.

Unholy Ghosts

HOLLOWAY

HE following story was recorded over a century ago by a Dr Spencer Hall, a much respected doctor, whose cousin living at Holloway and having adopted a baby girl, experienced the following phenomena:

'Philip and his first wife, Martha, who was a cousin of mine, having no children of their own, adopted the little daughter of a young woman who went to live at Derby. The child called them father and mother as soon as she could speak, not remembering her own parents – not even her mother. While yet very young, she one day began to cry out that there was a young woman looking at her, and wanting to come to her and according to her description of the person it must have been her mother. As no one else saw the apparition, Philip took her out of the house to that of a neighbour but the apparition kept them company, talking by the way. They then went to another house, where it accompanied them still, and seemed as though it wanted to embrace the child but at last vanished in the direction of Derby as the girl, now a young woman, describes it – in a flash of fire. Derby is about 14 miles distant from Holloway, and as in those days there was neither railway nor telegraph, communication between them was much slower than at present.

"As soon, however, as it was possible for intelligence to come, the news arrived that the poor child's mother had been burnt to death; that it happened about the time when it saw the apparition and, in short, that she was sorrowing and crying to be taken to the child during the whole time between being burnt and her expiration. This is no "idle ghost story", but a simple matter of fact, to which not only Philip, but all his old neighbours can testify and the young woman has not only related it more than once to me, but she told it in the same artless and earnest manner to my friend, the late Dr Samuel Brown, of Edinburgh, who once called at the cottage with me.'

DICKEY O'TUNSTEAD

'According to the evidence of many local inhabitants, the house is peaceful and quiet while the skull remains there, but if it be removed the noises recur, and a voice is heard in the wind as the latter, with strange moanings, comes through the keyholes of every door in the house, saying, "Fetch poor Dickey back. Fetch poor Dickey back." And to this day the weird skull rests in the quiet corner of the window, and in the room a peculiar silence reigns.'
J.Castle Hall.

Derbyshire's most famous ghost story is undoubtedly that of Dickey O'Tunstead. Dickey was a skull which once resided upon a windowsill in a farm that overlooked the Coombs Reservoir, between Chapel-en-le-Frith and Whaley Bridge, for over 360 years. According to the legend, of which there are several versions, the skull was that of a soldier named Ned Dickson, who, after returning from war in the 16th century to lay claim to his inheritance, was murdered by his cousin Jack and his wife, who cut off his head whilst he was sleeping, then buried the head near the farm, whilst the body was disposed of elsewhere. Soon after this terrible crime was committed strange happenings began to occur. Crops failed, cattle began to die, strange noises were heard and rumours of ghosts began to circulate in the district. Eventually the two cousins became frightened of these events and sought the advice of a local witch who advised them to 'dig up what the earth refused to hide', and give the totem a place of honour within the homestead. This they agreed to do and when they arrived back home they found the half-decayed head already in the farm, sitting on the kitchen windowsill 'as whan and as ghastly as when he was done'. The head remained with the couple for the rest of their lives, the skin and hair eventually rotting away to leave only the skull.

According to the legend the wife of the cousin that murdered Dickey was killed by a blow from her husband, later he met his own death when an oak tree fell, crushing the life out of him. A poem, one of many concerning Dickey, which was written by William Bennett earlier this century, tells of the fate of Dickey's murderers:

"What's that i'the nook, John?" she suddenly cried,
And shaking with terror they clearly espied
The head of Ned Dickson upright on the stone,
As whan and as ghastly as when he was done.

Many years passed away and the murderers fell,
By just retribution as ancient folk tell;
By a blow from her husband the woman was killed,
By the fall of an oak was Jack Johnson's blood
*   spilled.*

But the head of Ned Dickson still stood in the
*   nook,*
Though they tried to remove it by bell and by book;
Though wasted of skin and flesh, still the skull
Will remain at its post till its weird be full.

Other versions of the tale have it that the skull

At one time Dickey's reputation had grown so wide that they printed postcards of him sitting in his favourite window.

is that of one of two co-heiresses, who was brutally murdered by her sister for her share of the inheritance. On her deathbed the victim decreed that her bones should never be removed from the farm. Shortly after her death her ghost was seen walking the building and farmyard, from then on all manner of things began to go wrong. Farm labourers met with terrible accidents, cattle died of mysterious diseases, or wandered away, and terrible crying and screaming noises were frequently heard. The situation became so bad that eventually the evil co-heiress, recalling her sister's dying words, dug up her head and, taking it back to the farm, placed it on the windowsill. This story is perhaps closer to the truth as scientific tests carried out on the skull, early in the 20th century, revealed that Dickey is in fact a female. The name Dickey however has stuck and in 1809, a local historian wrote 'Why it should have been baptised with a name belonging to the male sex seems somewhat anomalous.'

The two legends do however, agree that if Dickey is removed from the farm all hell breaks loose. Hutchinson wrote that 'twice within the memory of man the skull has been taken from the premises once on building the present house on the site of the old one, and another time when it was buried in Chapel churchyard but there was no peace! no rest! it had to be replaced.'

Dickey O'Tunstead, Derbyshire's most famous ghost.

Once Dickey was thrown into the nearby Coombs Reservoir, but all the fish died. On another occasion the skull was thrown on a manure heap whilst the farm was being rebuilt, but each morning the workmen discovered that all the work carried out on the previous day had been undone, the same workmen also complained that strange low, growling noises could clearly be heard coming from the manure heap. The skull was reluctantly taken back out of the manure, and placed in a nearby barn on a large beam, the work was allowed to continue without further complications. When all the building work had been completed a party was had to celebrate, the skull screamed and caused such a commotion that it had to be taken back into the house and placed back on the windowsill.

Dickey also had a good side and would frequently help out on the farm. Those who showed him respect would accordingly be treated in the same way. He is said to have frequently drawn attention to animals who were ill or dying, cows that were calving and once screamed loudly when the farm was being burgled, drawing the attention of the sleeping farmer. On another occasion, a local man attempted to steal a sack of potatoes and lifting the sack on to his shoulder found that he could not move, he was frozen to the spot, meanwhile crockery in the farm kitchen was heard to rattle and shake, this in turn awoke the farmer who caught the thief. A passing waggoner once felt the ghostly wrath of Dickey when he saw a light on in the farm, window and laughingly commented that Dickey must be going to bed, the wagon he was driving immediately overturned.

Dickey's greatest success was over the London & North Western Railway Company, who in 1862 planned to build a bridge, linking Buxton with Whaley Bridge, across a piece of land that belonged to Tunstead Farm. Work for the bridge soon got under way, so did Dickey's ghost, for every time a foundation was laid, it sank further into the ground. Other problems occurred including, tools going missing, sections of the bridge

Coombs Reservoir, Chapel-en-le-Frith. Once Dickey's skull was thrown into the waters and all the fish died.

collapsing, workmen falling ill and rumours that the whole project was jinxed did little to help the situation. Eventually the whole project was abandoned and the bridge was built higher up the line at Dane Hay, now known as 'Dickey's Bridge'. One Lancashire dialect poet, Samuel Laycock, immortalised Dickey's antics when he wrote a poem entitled 'Address to Dickey', first published by the *Buxton Advertiser* in 1870:

> *Neaw, Dickie, be quiet Wi thee, lad*
> *An'let navvies an? railways a'be;*

> *Mon that shouldn't do soa, its too bad,*
> *What harm are they doin'to thee?*
> *Deed folk shouldn't meddle at o'*
> *But leov o'these matters to th'wick;*
> *They'll see ther're done gradely, aw know-*
> *Dos't'yer what aw say to thee, Dick?*

At one time Dickey's skull was exhibited for all to see, postcards were also available, unfortunately neither is the case today, Dickey's skull is now said to be bricked up behind a wall somewhere on the farm.

TUFA COTTAGE

THIS old keepers cottage stands midway along the Via Gellia and is built of a local porous stone which is formed by calcium carbonate which solidifies when water is deposited on to moss. Eventually the moss decays leaving this strange spongy looking stone, which is known commonly as Tufa. A wide variety of 'petrified' objects were once eagerly sought after by the Victorians. Matlock Bath houses a petrifying well, also said to be the haunt of a grey lady, with a wide variety of objects on display which have been calcified.

This charming house is reputed to be haunted

Tufa Cottage. The ghost of a woman with a knife sticking out of her back is reputed to haunt this charming house.

by the ghost of a woman who is seen with a large knife sticking out of her back. Via Gellia woods, located at the back of the house, have long been associated with black magic and witchcraft. Local children passing the house refer to it as the 'Witches House', because of its strange appearance. The house takes on a sinister profile when the moon rises in the evening.

Regardless of how the house may appear it is a charming building set in a most beautiful position. The appearance of the house has obviously given rise to its ghostly associations.

DICK TURPIN

THE GHOST of the notorious highwayman Richard Turpin is said to haunt several sites in Derbyshire and the Peak District. On stormy nights he can be seen riding across the Chevin at Belper, his cape blowing fiercely in the wind. He is also seen tending his beloved horse, Black Bess, outside several public houses. The Bull I' Th' Thorn, a 13th-century inn five miles south from Buxton, is said to be his favourite haunt.

The Bull I' Th' Thorn Public House. A favourite haunt of the notorious outlaw Dick Turpin.

At Heage he is seen with a pistol in his hand, whilst at Duffield he has been spotted perched in a tree. All the sightings of Dick have one thing in common, that the phantom highwayman has no face, and where eyes, nose, and mouth should be, there is only an empty shadowed hole.

In recent times there has been some debate as to where Dick Turpin was really born. His bones now rest at York, a city which firmly holds on to them. Some historians maintain a feeble claim that the notorious outlaw was born in Derbyshire. Some have even further demanded that his bones be returned to Derby. York, however, views the whole story of Dick Turpin ever having come from Derby as absolute rubbish, a pure invention by people simply seeking publicity.

Regardless of what happens to his bones, the notorious outlaw will still continue to haunt the lanes and woods of Derbyshire and the Peak District.

HEAGE HALL

HEAGE HALL once had a reputation for being one of the most haunted halls in Derbyshire. In centuries past villagers would not travel near the hall after darkness fell for fear of meeting something not of this world. A former resident and owner of the hall Mrs Arguile, committed suicide within one of the rooms there and, shortly afterwards, her ghost was seen by several people.

One such sighting came when a serving girl encountered the ghost of Mrs Arguile sitting behind her, watching what she was doing. Bessie, as the maid was known, died several weeks later, some say from the shock of what she had experienced.

Several decades later the hall was acquired by a gentleman known as Squire Pole, an unpleasant miser, who was so wretched to his wife, beating her and refusing her food, that she too eventually took her own life. Her ghost was also reputed to haunt the halls and corridors of the building. People who have seen her spectre report that she appears as miserable in death as she had been in life.

After the death of his wife Squire Pole is said to have become even more of a miser, taking to stashing his gold and silver in a huge iron-banded oak chest, upon which he placed 12 locks. When Squire Pole retired to his bed at night he put the chest next to his bed, placing upon it a loaded pistol and a razor sharp sword. The keys to the chest were fastened to a piece of string, which, in turn, was fastened to his wrist, the keys then being placed under his pillow. After his death the house came into the possession of two brothers named Shaw, who, according to local legend, found the misers treasure and melted it down at a nearby smithy then purchased another property in the village.

In the years that followed numerous people reported seeing Squire Pole's ghost which was said to, like the devil, take many forms. Once his ghost is said to have appeared as a black dog, another time he was seen with two black dogs wandering the local countryside, then he appeared as a big black bird and finally as a 'Shag-gard Foal'. Other reports state that he has been seen corpse-like driving a coach from Belper towards Heage.

Other reports of ghosts in the area of Heage, where they used to 'hang 'em in bunches', according to one local saying, include the appearance of Mary, Queen of Scots, Dick Turpin, a headless horseman and a white stage coach which has been seen trundling along the road near Heage Hall. A local to the area told me that in times past, according to her great-grandmother, it was believed that there existed a secret tunnel which led from Heage Hall to Wingfield Manor. The ghost of a white lady, seen near a local windmill is somehow connected to the secret tunnel, although the lady concerned could not remember the complete story her great-grandmother used to tell.

HEADLESS PHANTOMS

IN Derbyshire and the Peak District stories abound concerning headless phantoms, indeed the whole of British folklore is strewn with tales of these decapitated wraiths. Several experts of the supernatural suggest that the reason why there are so many headless ghosts is perhaps, due to the fact that in times past it was common practise to decapitate the dead in order to stop their spirits rising from the grave. Archaeological excavations of many Pagan, Celtic, and Saxon burials have revealed that the heads of some of the remains found have been removed, then placed between their knees or feet.

Many of the headless phantoms are male; more are female, some are dogs and a few are horses. Various ghosts carry their dismembered heads under their arms, while others are completely without a head, like the ghost of a lady that haunts the Quiet Woman public house at Earl Sterndale, south-west of Buxton. The locals tell the story of a former landlord of the pub who, several centuries ago, cut off his wife's head to stop her continuous nagging. The man then gave himself up and confessed his crime. The people of the village, instead of punishing him, took pity on the landlord and forgave him for his sin as they knew that the woman had indeed, been a terrible shrew. To this day, upon the signboard for this popular watering hole, are the assurances, 'Soft Word's Turneth Away Wrath'. Another headless ghost haunts the house and grounds of Stoke Hall at Grindleford, (see Fair Flora).

Shady Lane, close to Thornbridge Hall, at Ashford-in-the-Water, is a place where at midnight one may encounter the ghosts of '12 headless men', carrying an empty coffin. Should you be unlucky enough to meet the gruesome cortège you may well find yourself occupying the empty coffin.

At Ashover Church there is said to be a 'headless woman' who haunts the churchyard. Much debate surrounds the headless phantom and there is a great deal of speculation as to who she might be. This particular headless lady was last recorded as being seen in 1890 when she was spotted in the north isle of the church at 8pm by a local. To the south of Ashover Village is Stub-

ben Edge Hall where a human skull was once unearthed when alterations were being made to the building. A popular belief at the time was that the skull had been taken from Ashover churchyard, as part of a wager 20 years earlier. Locals believed that the headless phantom haunted the churchyard, apparently looking for her stolen head.

One of the Peak District's most fearsome headless spectres is to be found riding a white fiery steed through the Manifold Valley on moonlit nights. One local gentleman who saw the ghost in the 1930s describes the spectre as 'a man on a horse without a yed on, an awful gory sight!' According to the legend two local men once murdered a peddler and chopped off his head. Then, sitting his body upon a horse they forced it to ride across the moors. Another version of the tale tells how a knight was killed then decapitated by the Scots, his faithful soldiers then carried the headless corpse home.

THE MINERS ARMS PUBLIC HOUSE, EYAM

BUILT during the early years of the 17th century, shortly before the village was ravaged by the bubonic plague, the Miners Arms at Eyam is a fine example of what a village pub should be. This ancient inn was once used by the Great Barmote Court which met annually, consisting of lead miners who settled claims and grievances between themselves. Now functioning as a bed and breakfast, the Miners Arms offers a warmth and charm which appears to be all too often lacking in many modern day establishments.

A plaque within the building states that this property is the most haunted building within the village, a claim which the present landlord declares and believes to be true. The building has a long history of being haunted by several spirits,

although I was informed that the most frequent spook which manifests itself does so in the form of footsteps or running, being frequently heard on the upper landing of the building.

Several people who have stayed at the pub have reported seeing and hearing strange happenings, so frightened were one couple that they refused to stay another night within the building. The couple had apparently woken in the early hours of the morning to find the room filled with what appeared to be old fashioned medical equipment. Thinking it strange, but too tired from a previous day's journeying, the couple went back to sleep. On arising some hours later the pair discovered to their surprise that the equipment they had seen was no longer there. So frightened were the couple by their experience that they immediately settled their bill and left. The story of their brush with the supernatural only came to light when the landlady from another bed and breakfast, which the couple had fled to, came to eat at the Miners Arms and reiterated her story to the staff on duty.

The Miners Arms, Eyam. Said to be the most haunted building in the village.

A former parish council chairman reported seeing an elderly lady dressed in an old fashioned style bonnet with jet sequins, sporting a cape and side elasticated boots, enter the building after it had been newly altered and refurbished. The council chairman followed the wraith into the building and watched her as she confusedly wandered the building before she vanished before his eyes. Many people believe that this ghost is the former wife of a landlord who had murdered her by throwing her down the stairs in a mad fit of anger, this apparently took place in the 17th century.

THE DEVIL'S ELBOW

HAIRPIN Bend, often referred to as the 'Devils Elbow', is located on a minor road which connects Glossop with Woodhead. According to an ancient legend two young lovers once made a pact with the Devil, later they regretted their decision and informed the evil fiend that they would not hold to it. His Satanic Majesty, furious at being double crossed, gave chase to the two young lovers. As they raced across the moors the Devil soon gained on them and, lifting his arm to strike them dead with a thunder bolt, the devil froze as out of the skies appeared a strange light from within which boomed a voice which spoke one word "Hold". At which point the Devil's arm froze as simultaneously the two young lovers vanished, along with the strange light. The story told by Thomas Middleton in 1906 adds that the lovers 'were made perfectly happy by the fairies, and that they still haunt the banks of the Etherow at certain seasons of the year in the forms of two white swans. As for the devil he received a shock. At the moment the light appeared, his right arm had been bent at the elbow for the purpose of seizing hold of his prey, But lo! when his victims had disappeared, he found that the powers that had delivered them from him had turned his right arm into stone. Not a muscle of it could he move, it would not bend, it was worse than useless he tore the arm out by the roots and left it there – the elbow showing prominently over Longdendale.

The Devil's Elbow is also said to be the haunt of a solitary Roman Soldier, who has been seen wandering the nearby lonely moors. Other ghosts include strange phantom lights seen flickering and dancing along the road, a huge slug like creature with one eye which was seen by a

local man returning home one night and a hooded figure experienced by a woman passing through the vicinity.

The whole countryside and moors about the Devil's Elbow region has long had a reputation for being a stronghold of pagan worship. Rum–ours abound concerning witches and demons, earlier this century Thomas Middleton described how Longdendale 'has always been noted for the number of its inhabitants devoted to the study of magic arts.' Mossey Lea, near Glossop was also according to Middleton, 'notable as having been the home of a great magician who dwelt there in the olden time, who was renowned far and wide – he was perhaps, the most powerful and learned of all magicians since the time of Merlin.' The story reiterates how the magician's reputation grew so much that the local people referred to him as Dr Faust, after the famous German sorcerer. One day the Devil was passing and paid Dr Faust a visit, the conversation grew heated and the devil challenged the magician to a race across a Roman road on the moors. Thinking his powers would be great enough Dr Faust accept-ed. The race began and before very long the Devil was getting the better of him. Realising that his horse would never beat his Satanic Majesty, he pushed the animal forward faster, aware that just up ahead there existed a stream. On arriving at the small stretch of water, he jumped it in the knowledge that evil has not the power to pass pure running water – Faust had managed to

The Devil's Elbow. His Satanic Majesty is reputed to be responsible for causing this dangerous bend in the road.

outwit the devil. Realising what the clever magician had done, Satan screamed a scream that shook the very foundations of the earth and passing the countryside north of Snake Pass, he scratched a huge gash on the moors which, from that day to this is known as the Devil's Dyke. The Roman road along which the two had raced, between Brough and Melandra at Glossop, is to this day known as the Doctor's Gate, after the legend of the magician and the devil.

Tales from the Crypt

LUD'S CHURCH

THIS dramatic grit-stone rock chasm, close to the border, where Derbyshire, Staffordshire and Cheshire meet, near the village of Wincle, hidden in the Back Forest, also known as 'The Haunted Forest', abounds in tales of the supernatural for, according to legend it is here that the Green Knight, of Arthurian legend, was slew by Sir Gawain. Originally it was thought that Thor's Cave at Wetton Mill, also known as Thurshole, or Nan Tor, was the original site of the Green Chapel. The scholar, Mabel Day was one of the first to spot the similarities between this ancient cave site and the famous Middle English poem.

Lud's Church, or, The Green Chapel, as it is often referred to, is undoubtedly the result of a landslide caused by a fault in the rock. Extending about 220ft into the hillside, being 50ft deep, 9ft wide with steep stone steps which lead down into the dark recesses of the earth, Lud's Church, is undoubtedly a spooky place. Tales of witches, goblins and fairy folk abound, for it is here on moonlit nights that one may experience these creatures of supernatural origins dancing and worshipping the gods of old.

The ghost of a bearded man has been seen at the entrance to the cave and I am informed that it is probably the spirit of Walter de Ludauk, a follower of Robert Wycliff, a heretical preacher who, in the 15th century, was known to have held secret religious services at the cave until he

Lud's Church, also known as the 'Green Chapel' of Arthurian legend. The ghost of a bearded man and a 'white lady', known as Lady Lud, haunt this natural cave.

was captured with the majority of his followers by government troops. According to legend Robert Wycliff's granddaughter was killed in the skirmish, buried somewhere near the entrance to the cave after which, for many years, a statue known as 'Lady Lud', stood close by the entrance. Lady Lud is also said to haunt the area around the cave entrance.

The name Lud could also be derived from one of the legendary kings of Britain, a descendant of Brutus, Lud, who gave his name to London, Lud's Town and Ludgate Hill near Fleet Street.

Others maintain that the name Lud is derived from the Celtic sun god Lugh the Lamfada, which in Gaelic means the 'Long Handed', or the 'Far Shooter'.

THE GHOST OF BEN STILES

HARPUR Hill, near Buxton, was once reputed to be haunted by the ghost of a man named Ben Stiles. A murder took place on a heath near a place called the Frith, where an old stile once stood. According to William Turner writing in 1901, 'the poor victim was named Ben and, in absence of a surname, he has been dubbed Stiles by the country people, owing to the fact that his body was found at or near this particular stile.'

Not long after his body was found reports began to emerge that his ghost had appeared to several locals. Other reports record how his ghost would appear at sunset till sunrise, whilst another historian claimed that the ghost of Ben Stiles could only be seen by those people possessing the gift of second sight.

LOVERS' LEAPS

DERBYSHIRE has several 'Lover's Leaps'. There is one near Buxton, one at Winster, one at Matlock and another at Dovedale. All of the lover's leaps have, at some point in time, been said to be haunted. Many versions of the tales exist, the following are perhaps the most commonly known.

Buxton

Not too far from Buxton, near to Ashwood Dale, is a hill which is known locally as the Lover's Leap. The story connected to the hill concerns two young lovers who, forbidden to marry by their parents, decided one dark night to elope to Peak Forest, which was in times passed, a Gretna Green of Derbyshire.

Setting out after dusk, when they thought they would least be missed, the two lovers stole away on horseback and, by the light of a full moon, they made their escape. The two had not travelled far when, from behind them, came the clatter of horses and riders, they were being pursued! Their parents, discovering that the two had gone missing, had sent a party of local men to bring them back. Being determined not to be caught they pushed their horses harder into a fast gallop and when the girl's horse lost a shoe she mounted her partner's horse and they rode on together.

As they reached the top of a hill they could see a large gap yawning before them. In one last desperate bid to get away, they pushed their horse even harder and, reaching the gap, they leapt into oblivion, just managing to land safely on the other side. Their pursuers, reaching the gap, stopped and turned back, afraid that they would not make the jump, the lovers rode on into the night and on reaching Peak Forest they were married, after which like all good love stories they lived happily ever after.

On certain nights of the year a re-enactment of the frenzied chase is still said to be heard, or seen, upon the hillside near Ashwood Dale. Other tales tell of a phantom coach and horses also seen in the district.

Winster Hall, where two young lovers threw themselves to their deaths.

Winster Hall

Built in the middle of the 18th century, from gritstone brought from Stancliffe quarries in Darley Dale, an earlier house dating from the reign of James I, is said to have existed on the site before the present building was built. The hall was once owned by Llewellyn Jewitt, a famous antiquarian and collector of Derbyshire folklore and legends.

The hall is haunted by the ghosts of two young lovers who were forbidden to marry. The young gentleman was a coachman and the girl was the daughter of the house. Their falling in love caused a great deal of embarrassment, especially to the girl's parents who had already arranged for her to be married to another. The night before the arranged marriage was due to take place the two would-be lovers climbed to the roof of the house and, clasping each other

tightly, flung themselves over the balustrade to their stoney deaths. Since that fateful day Winster Hall has been known as a 'Lover's Leap', one of the four in Derbyshire.

The hall has for many years had a reputation for being haunted, many reports abound of a white lady seen wandering the hall and grounds. Other stories tell of a re-enactment of the death of the two young lovers, this is said to take place near Christmas each year.

Dovedale

The story concerning the Lover's Leap at Dovedale is now long forgotten although, the lofty tor of that name, is still referred to by locals as a Lover's Leap. The story is said to be similar to that of Winster Hall, two young lovers, forbidden to marry, climb the rock and leap to

Lover's Leap, Stoney Middleton. The ghost of the unfortunate Hannah Baddaley can still be seen here.

their deaths. There forever afterwards to haunt the rocks which took their lives.

Stoney Middleton

In 1762, Hannah Baddaley, being one of the prettiest girls in the area, was eagerly sought after by many a young man. Hannah finally chose to be wooed by a handsome young man named William Barnsley, who courted her for almost a year. The young couple were very happy until, eventually William lost interest and told Hannah he no longer wished to see her.

Devastated by his rejection Hannah ran to an 80ft cliff at Middleton Dale and threw herself off the top. Instead of plunging to her death the wind caught her petticoats making them billow out like a parachute and she glided to the bottom of the precipice where she landed in some thorn bushes. The only injury she suffered were a few cuts and bruises caused by the bushes and rocks at the base of the cliff.

Two years after she had attempted to take her own life Hannah Baddaley died, some say from a broken heart, aged 26 years, she was buried in a local churchyard.

A ghostly re-enactment of her fateful jump is still said to take place, some people of the district say her ghost can be seen, looking fragile and pale, wandering on the hillside where she originally attempted to take her own life.

DUFFIELD CHURCH

ST ALKMUND'S CHURCH at Duffield contains architecture of the 12th and 15th centuries. In the chapel is a fine alabaster tomb, dated 1536, upon which are the effigies of Sir Roger Mynors and his wife. Of particular interest is a wall monument dedicated to Anthony Bradshaw, his two wives and their 20 children. He had the tomb made 14 years before he died. However, by the time he did die, he had managed to father a further three children. He was a great uncle of Judge John Bradshaw, who presided at the trials of Charles I, Anthony Bradshaw later founded four almshouses at Duffield, these were pulled own in the last century.

Very few churches in England can lay claim to the fact that Satan himself chose the spot on which the church should be built, Duffield Church is one such building. According to an ancient legend the site of the church was chosen to be near to where Duffield Castle once stood. The materials for the church were going to be part provided by the remains of the old castle which once belonged to the de Ferrers family who were at one time the Earls of Derby.

Preparation for the commencement of the church had taken place and the builders had already started to lay the first stones. On returning to the site the following day the workmen discovered all of their previous work had been dismantled and the materials moved to a different location at the other end of the village. Thinking it strange that such a thing should happen the workmen brought back the materials and recommenced the building work. When they next returned to the site the same thing had hap-

Duffield Church. Said to have been moved by the devil.

pened again. This time solemn prayers were said over the bricks and mortar for it was now believed that the devil himself, was responsible for moving the building materials. Once again they attempted to build the church only to find that the same thing happened again. This continued for a week until eventually, ground down by the situation, they gave up and built the church where it may still be seen today, by the side of the River Derwent, at the opposite end of the village from where it was originally intended.

From that time onwards it was firmly believed by the people of the village that evil spirits occupied, or often met at, the site where the church was intended to be built. For several centuries stories were told about the 'Brown Man', boggart or bogey, which was said to be seen every night near to where the castle once existed. Very few people would venture there after the edge of darkness, for fear of meeting the arch-fiend. Another version of the legend tells how his Satanic Majesty did not wish the church to inhabit an exalted position on the hillside for fear that it would attract too much attention, therefore it might have attracted too many customers.

DALE ABBEY

IN 1155 Serlo de Grendon, Lord of the Dale, invited some Austin canons from Calke Abbey to establish a colony at Depedale, as the area of Dale Abbey was known then. The Abbey became successful and within time a wealthy community of friars flourished there. After several years the canons became more obsessed with themselves than their spirituality and improvement of their minds. They would frequently take to the Royal forest making merry and hunting the royal sport, until the king heard of their transgressions and

Dale Abbey Hermit's Cave. Phantom cries and screaming can be heard coming from this ancient carved out cave.

ordered that they should leave an account of their hunting, whereupon they resigned from the priory and returned to Calke Abbey.

For some time the priory remained closed until William de Grendon, son of Serlo, invited another group of canons, from the Abbey of Tupholme in Lincolnshire, to establish a fresh community at Dale. The new canons, having no land to support them, only stayed at the priory for seven years. When the priory was given up, Henry, the prior, refused to leave, and eventually absconded. Later it was discovered that he had been involved in counterfeiting money and he was found to be having a relationship with a common working girl from Morley, in whose company he was eventually found, then taken back by force to Tupholme. Not long after Friar Henry had arrived back at Tupholme, he was discovered to have committed suicide by cutting his wrists whilst taking a hot bath.

After another unsuccessful attempt to establish an abbey at Dale, Geoffrey de Salicosa Mara and his wife Matilda, gave the village of Stanley to the Premonstratensian order and joined it with Dale thus making it financially stronger. Under the supervision of a new Abbot the abbey grew and eventually became one of the most successful abbeys of its day. By the time of the dissolution the abbey owned property in Derby, Nottingham, Alvaston, Hilton, Breaston, Kirk Hallam, Codnor, Ilkeston and many other towns and villages.

On 30th October 1538, Dale Abbey and all its possessions were handed over to the crown. Not too long after this the abbey was razed to the ground and its fabric was used in the construction of several of the cottages and farmhouses in the village. Today very little remains of the abbey except the great arch of the chancel window, the ground plan of the abbey church can also be clearly seen, whilst at Morley Church two of the refectory windows have been incorporated into the building. At Radbourne Church, a few miles west of Derby, there survives several benches and bench ends from the abbey church.

The ghost story concerning Dale Abbey begins over 800 years ago, an ancient manuscript by a canon named Thomas de Muscova now in the British Museum chronicles the history of Dale Abbey including the events of the life of a Derby baker who, being very compassionate, for many years gave presents of food and clothing from the Church of St Mary's to the poor.

One night in a dream, the Blessed Virgin Mary appeared to the baker informing him that, 'Acceptable in the eyes of my son and of me, are the alms thou hast bestowed. But now, if thou art willing to be made perfect, leave all that though hast, and go to Depedale, where thou shalt serve my son and me in solitude and when though shalt happily terminated thy course, thou shalt inherit the kingdom of love, joy, and eternal bliss which God has prepared for those who love him.'

When he woke up he thanked God and the Virgin Mary and immediately set out to look for Depedale. Travelling east he soon came upon the village of Stanley, where he heard a woman say to her daughter: "Take our calves with you: drive them as far as Depedale, and make haste back." Hearing this the baker knew that God was indirectly instructing him on where to go, so, he followed the young maiden to Depedale. On arriving there he was horrified to find that the area was a marshy inhospitable domain. Feeling inspired by God, he felt strangely drawn to travel south-east of Depedale, where he came upon a hillside which was made of sandstone. At once he set about cutting a cave in the rock and, within a short time, he had made himself a dwelling.

Some weeks after he had made his home in the cave, Ralph Fitz Geremund, the Lord of Ockbrook and Alvaston, was hunting deer with several other members of nobility when he saw smoke coming from the hermit's cave. He was angry that anyone should dare to live in Depedale without his permission, the penalties being severe for anyone who broke them. On reaching the cave he found the hermit dressed in rags of sackcloth and animal skins. Lord

Dale Abbey Ruins. The tragic figure of a monk who committed suicide haunts the ruins and the surrounding area.

Geremund demanded to know why the hermit was trespassing on his property. When he heard the explanation he became moved by the story and granted to him the site of his cell as well as the tithe of a mill at Alvaston, which would support him in his spiritual quest. Shortly after being granted the mill, the hermit began to build himself a chapel and oratory near a spring westward of the cave he had cut for himself.

Several decades after the hermit had built his new oratory, which eventually became a monastery, a notorious highway robber named Uthlagus happened to be passing with his band of outlaws. Deciding to settle for the night on top of the hill where the hermit's cave was, it was not long before they were all fast asleep. During the night Uthlagus had a dream in which he saw rising from the earth a golden cross rising into the sky where the monastery stood. When he awoke he immediately roused the others and told them his dream. His accomplices, believing what he said to be an act of tomfoolery laughed, at which Uthlagus became angry stating that the valley below was a holy place and that one day men from all nations would go there on pilgrimage. Without further hesitation Uthlagus packed his belongings and kissing each of his criminal accomplices goodbye, he went down into the valley and lived out his remaining days

in the carved out cave as a hermit. Thus it was that by the middle of the 12th century the area of Dale Abbey had received a holy reputation.

On many occasions locals from the village of Dale Abbey have reported seeing the figure of a ghostly monk wandering the area around the abbey. Many of the houses in the village border what was once the abbey and its gardens. There are also reports of chanting being heard coming from the area of where the abbey would have stood. Frequent too are the reports of a hooded monk seen standing near the great chancel arch. The hermit's cave is also known to be haunted by several ghosts, one local lady, whilst walking her dog in the vicinity of the cave one evening distinctly heard crying noises coming from within the carved out cave. On investigating the strange noised she found the cave to be completely empty, her dog appeared quite apprehensive and turning to walk away she distinctly heard a male voice call her name. So frightened was she by the experience that she now refuses to venture anywhere near the cave as she is convinced the site is haunted.

The ghost of the monk seen in the area is believed to be that of Prior Henry, who, having taken his own life, is doomed to wander the face of the earth as guardian of the ruins, until judgement day.

INFIDELS' CEMETERY

LYING alongside a narrow strip of road between Ashford-in-the-Water and Monsal Head can be found a small neglected 19th-century cemetery. Most of the stones are tumbled now, a high wall crumbling with decay hides their sorry state from passing prying eyes. The late Clarence Daniel recorded that none of the gravestones were inscribed with any reference to God, the Bible or Jesus. Thus the name Infidels' Cemetery became

the title associated with the cemetery. People once believed that the occupants of the tombs were buried there because they were in some way evil, there is no evidence whatsoever for this being the case, but perhaps this accounts for the location having a reputation for being haunted. Other reports infer that the people buried at the cemetery were probably a small local community of Baptists, this seems a little more likely.

Local children used to tell stories concerning

Infidels' Cemetery. Once believed to be the burial place of evil people.

a vampire, which they believed frequented the site, other stories, told by the locals concern the ghost of a grey lady who has been seen wandering between the gravestones at dusk. A third ghost is that of a man who appears just outside the entrance to the cemetery, dressed in black, he eventually turns and disappears through the wall into the cemetery, although anyone following him will find only themselves in this dark and lonely spot.

ASHOVER CHURCH

SET amidst fine moorlands and residing within the Amber Valley, between Chesterfield and Matlock, is the village of Ashover. The village church of All Saints, which is mentioned in the Doomsday book, is believed to be of national importance as it houses a rare lead font of which there are said to be only 30 or so in the country. It is fitting that the font should be found at Ashover as lead was mined locally since Roman times. There are many other interesting features to be seen at the church including a fine carved alabaster tomb, dated 1511, with effigies of Thomas Babington and his wife Edith,

on the sides of the tomb are carved mourners, angels and saints, which was said by Pevsner to be the best of its date in Derbyshire.

The church, according to many people, is said to be haunted by the headless spectre of a woman. The phantom was last officially reported to have been seen in 1890, when the ghost was sighted in the north aisle of the church at eight o'clock one evening. There is much speculation as to who the ghost might be. Many villagers who are familiar with the ghost story believe the headless lady to be a local who was bludgeoned to death with a hammer, by her husband, John Towndrow, a farmer, in 1841, who then cut off her head and then finally cut his own throat. He was later buried in the churchyard with all his clothes on at 9 o'clock at night, with no shoes on, after a verdict by a local jury.

Another story concerns a skull which was uncovered at Stubben Edge Hall, just south of the village, during the construction of a conservatory in 1879. The skull was said to have been carried there by a local lad who, as part of a wager, had taken the skull from Ashover churchyard. As a consequence to this desecration, the ghost of the skull's owner is said to have abandoned the grave and haunt the churchyard as a reminder to all those who would steal from the dead.

An empty stone coffin at the church is also believed to be haunted and anyone wishing to hear the rattling of ghostly chains must walk round the empty coffin three times and then lie within it with your eyes closed, you will soon hear the strange sounds at first faint and as you lie there the noises will gather in momentum. Many locals informed me that they had indeed tried this and heard the sound of the chains.

ALDERWASLEY

UPON a hillside and not too far from Matlock Bath lies the quiet hamlet of Alderwasley. The present chapel dedicated to St Margaret, now doubling as the local community centre, has for many years been said to be haunted. Strange singing has been heard to emanate from the empty building late at night and villagers living near to the chapel report hearing bells ring and strange shuffling noises. On visiting Alderwasley village I enquired of several of the villagers, some of which lived near to the chapel, if they had heard the strange ghostly sounds which are said to flow from the building. Alas none that I asked seemed to know much about the ghosts except one gentleman who said that although he was familiar with the stories he had not heard of any active haunting within the chapel for some time.

Clarence Daniel, author of several local ghost books records that 'Such a village ought to be haunted, for it has a field called Killcroft and a farm with the lugubrious name of Buryhill Farm, place names which must have been born out of some sinister circumstances in the past.'

A much older building is believed to have occupied the site of the chapel before the present one was built, it is further thought that the carvings incorporated into the walls of the chapel date from this earlier building. The carvings which can be seen today consist of con-

An ancient Sheela-na-gig at Alderwasley Church. These blatant Pagan sexual symbols appear to be synonymous with buildings being haunted.

Alderwasley Church. Strange eerie music was once heard emanating from the empty church.

torted faces and grimacing masks. By far the most interesting carving is that of a 'Sheela-na-gig', an ancient fertility symbol or, as some people prefer to call them, a piece of medieval pornography. Such blatant sexual symbols date back to a time when ancient man still half held on to the old religion of Paganism and perhaps in the spiritual confusion of the time were allowed to incorporate some of the older gods into their doctrines of belief. This would have been allowed and tolerated by the then elders of the Christian church for they knew that to irradiate the old gods would not have been that easy by commandment alone, so why not partially adopt and then eventually remove completely.

DERWENT WATER — A SERMON FOR THE DEAD

THE following ghost story was once very popular amongst the people of the Peak District in the earlier part of the last century. There are several churches to which this story applies although the most famed setting for the story seems to centre around a church at Derwent Woodlands, which now lies beneath the waters of the Ladybower Reservoir.

Several centuries ago, in many parts of the Peak District, superstitious people believed that on the first Sunday after Christmas anyone brave enough to stay in a church, when the clock struck midnight, would see a ghostly procession of the spirits of those that were going to die in the village in the following year, pass into the church to be blessed. The most popular version of the story concerns a young parson who was appointed to the parish church of Derwent Woodlands. He was not a local man, nor was he a stranger to Derbyshire having been a curate in the south of the county. The people of the parish made him welcome and did all they could to make life as easy for him as possible. The new curate did not lack enthusiasm and the locals found him to be a breath of fresh air. One of the reasons that he had accepted his new position was that his health had not been altogether good, the new curate hoped that the clean air of the high northern hills would do his weak chest and bronchitic cough some good.

Several months passed by and all seemed to be going well, the people of the parish had accepted the young curate and found it quite refreshing to have someone who was keenly interested in their village lifestyles and old fashioned ways. Then one evening after a service one of the wardens of the church asked the new curate if he would perform an age old service for the people of the parish, who had nominated the warden, to ask the curate if he would perform a sermon for the dead on their behalf. The curate was furious and sent them away stating that he would have no part in such a superstitious, non-Christian ceremony, which he knew the bishop would forbid, furthermore having its roots set in pagan religious beliefs made it an unthinkable thing to do.

The year drew on and the curate noticed that the attitude of his parishioners had slightly changed towards him, seeming less trusting of him now, he often caught them looking curiously at him and he knew exactly what they was thinking, they were curious to whether he would perform the sermon for the dead or not. He, however, was adamant that he was going to have nothing to do with such a sermon and continued with his usual duties hoping that the villagers would forget about their bizarre request and not mention it again.

On the first Sunday after Christmas the people of the parish filed into church and took up their places to listen to the service. The vicar looked about him and noticed that many of the faces held an expectant look upon them. Knowing that they were curious as to whether he would give the sermon for the dead, the vicar deliberately preached about the foolishness of superstitious belief and how important it was to remain within the teachings of the Christian church if redemption and life eternal was to be granted to all in the life hereafter.

The service finished, the congregation dispersed and went home, many of them disappointed that the vicar had chosen not to give a sermon for the dead. Returning to the vicarage, the curate decided that he would return to the church at midnight to prove that the superstition was just nonsense.

A few minutes to midnight the vicar made his way into the church and stood in the pulpit waiting for the church clock to strike midnight. On the first chime of the clock, the vicar thought he saw movement at the back of the church but quickly convinced himself that it must be the poor lighting playing tricks on his eyes. The clock continued to chime and at the last stroke of midnight a breeze seemed to move through the church and out of thin air appeared the wraiths of 15 people or more who seemed to gaze at the vicar expectantly.

Realising that he had been wrong the vicar looked at the forlorn faces before him, in horror his eyes came to rest on a figure before him which he immediately recognised to be his own. His eyes filling with tears the vicar knew that it was the will of God. The faces of the spirits were so sad in their appearance, so forlorn and tired that the vicar took pity and began to speak asking that God may take pity on those before him and grant them peace in the next life. One by one the wraiths filed before him and each he gave a blessing to, until the last one had been served, then to turn from him and vanish into the shadows.

Winter passed to spring and the vicar's health grew increasingly worse. The parishioners who had first viewed him with suspicion, grew to love him like one of their own and he came to be one of the most respected vicars ever to grace their parish church. Finally, when his death came, the people of the village of Derwent Woodlands were devastated and deeply mourned their loss. When the vicar's last moments came he was not surprised to die. He had known that it was to be his last year of life for he had seen what few mortals have seen, a gathering of souls destined for a better place and proof in the greater wisdom of God.

ST PETER'S CHURCH, HOPE

THE OLDEST PLACE of Christian worship in the northern Peak District is St Peter's Church at Hope, near Hathersage, which was at one time one of the largest parishes in England. According to the Domesday survey of 1086 the parish included Fairfield (Buxton), Tideswell, Woodlands, Chapel-en-le-Frith, Stoke, Foolow and Nether Padley. The present day church (1200-1400), is thought to have been built on the site of an older Norman and Saxon church. A most interesting Saxon cross within the churchyard dates from the time of King Alfred and was hidden for many years,

St Peter's Church, Hope. The oldest place of Christian worship in North Derbyshire, where the spirits of the ancient dead are not at rest.

from the time of Cromwell, in the fabric of the first village school, until 1850.

The exterior of the church shows many traces of earlier beliefs and one need only look closely at the ornate carved gargoyles to see how influenced the stonemasons were by superstitions and the older pagan beliefs. When I visited Hope Parish Church I was told an interesting story by the vicar, the tale concerns a grotesque carved stone head above the main entrance to the church. The head, according to the vicar, had only returned to the church in recent years having spent several decades in another part of the country, taken there by a gentleman who was at one time a villager who had worked on the church in his youth, taken a shine to the head and removed it. At the time the head was lying idle and nobody seemed to want it, so he took it with him.

As the years passed the gentleman concerned moved away from the village to another part of the country. The son of the gentleman concerned, having grown up travelled to the village of his father's youth on a sightseeing holi-day and whilst there reiterated to the vicar the story concerning the head. The vicar searched all records to see if there was any mention of the head but could find none. Both parties agreed that it would be best for the head to be returned to its original home and, after several months, the head was indeed returned and set into its new position where it can be seen today.

The head appears to be from a time before the present church was built, probably from a collection of Celtic heads for such heads were gathered by the Celtic priests and worshipped, even today there are still cults which continue to worship heads in Derbyshire and the Peak District. If the head is from an earlier time, then the Church is surely built on a much earlier site, probably of Druidic or Pagan association.

Several ghosts are said to haunt the church-yard, the two most prolific being the ghosts of an old man and woman. One group of youths I came upon informed me that a vampire freq-uented the graveyard but this was probably just a tale that local children tell.

ILAM HALL

THE HALL WAS presented to the National Trust in 1934 by Sir Robert McDougall as a Youth Hostel. Much of the original hall was demolished when the hall became a hostel although what remains is still very impressive.

The church, located within the grounds of Ilam Hall, is of Norman origin and, like the hall, was rebuilt during the 19th century managing to save and incorporate some of the original Norman stonework. There are several memorials within the church including Robert Meverell of Throwley Hall (1625), whose daughter married Thomas, Lord Cromwell. A very fine example of Francis Chantry's work depicting David Pike Watts on his death bed, surrounded by his grandchildren and daughter, can also be found within the church. The grounds of the hall are also worth exploring, not just for the beauty of the grounds but also for the ghosts which are said to haunt certain areas of the woodland. Not far from the hall is a grotto where the 17th-century dramatist William Congreve wrote his comedy *The Old Bachelor*, his stone desk and chair is still there for all to see.

The hall is said to be haunted by a white lady who has also been seen wandering the Italian Gardens. One lady, called Angela, who stayed at the Youth Hostel several years ago, informed me that a white lady was in the habit of waking people up in the middle of the night and has also

Ilam Hall. The haunt of a white lady, a phantom coach and horses and a one-time resting place of a saint.

been seen wandering the hallways and corridors within the building. Also said to haunt the exterior of the hall is a phantom coach and horses which has frequently been seen turning around in one of the old courtyards, although no one seems to know why this ghostly visitation takes place, or indeed, if ever there was an accident concerning a coach and horses, and if there was, is the white lady in some way associated with it.

Perhaps the most interesting feature of Ilam church is the tomb of Saint Bertram, sometimes Betelin, believed to be the son of a Staffordshire prince. At an early age Bertram had decided to travel to Ireland and during his journey he met, fell in love with and married a beautiful Irish princess. The father of the bride was infuriated by the union, so the couple decided that it would be best to flee Ireland and return to Mercia in order to escape the King's wrath.

The young princess had fallen pregnant and being in an advanced state of gestation the long perilous journey was made slower. Arriving at what is today Ilam, which was at that time part of a great forest, the princess went into labour. Bertram, not knowing what to do, decided that he would seek out a midwife and hastily made a shelter out of sticks and evergreen shrubs before leaving his wife. Whilst he was away the baby was born, but alas, the woods were home to ferocious

*Saint Bertram's Tomb at Ilam Church.
Miracles are still said to happen here.*

Ilam Church seen from the Italian Gardens. The wraith of a 'White Lady' is seen to wander between the church and the gardens.

wolves and sensing that the princess and baby were vulnerable the wolves pounced. Although the princess put up a fight, in her weakened condition she could not fight them off for long, eventually she was overcome and the wolves devoured both mother and child.

Returning with the midwife Bertram discovered the mutilated bodies of his wife and child. From that moment onwards Bertram became a hermit and immediately took himself away to a place of isolation. Only once during his years as a hermit did he leave his holy solitude, shortly after his father's death, to raise an army to defeat his father's enemies, aided it is told by the mighty presence of an angel.

Saint Bertram, as he became, is believed to have died around AD110. Within his lifetime he is said to have performed many miracles, including healing the sick and driving out demons. Even after his death the hermitage became a place of pilgrimage, still miracles were said to happen, especially if water was taken from a holy well bearing his name, near which a sacred ash tree grew. Today people still travel to Ilam to seek out what has become known as 'Bertram's Tomb', located within a small chapel inside the church of The Holy Cross. Masses of cards, requests and flowers adorn the top of the tomb, and although Saint Bertram's remains are no longer in the tomb, they were moved to Stafford, some people still believe that some holy essence from his earthly body still remains.

A FAMOUS VISITATION

PERHAPS the most famous ghost story to have come out of Ashbourne is a ghost story that concerns the late Diana Dors who, in 1962, was appearing at a show in Ashbourne in aid of St Monica's Church of England Childrens' Home.

The actress had retired to bed in the 16th-century cottage she was staying at, the building being several miles west of Ashbourne. She had not been asleep long when she was disturbed from her slumber only to find that she was not alone in her room. Miss Dors awoke to see an apparition of an aged man standing in her room. She described him as being haggard with long flowing hair, she later gave an interview with a local newspaper in which she stated that she had been very frightened.

After her experience locals informed Diana that she had probably seen the ghost of a Jacobite soldier who had been killed in 1745 during the year that Bonnie Prince Charlie and his Highlanders had advanced as far as Derby before turning back. Locals also informed Diana that several of the Highlanders had been apprehended by King George's troops and executed in the area, this idea apparently felt comfortable to the renowned actress, and she is said to have believed that the long-haired apparition she had seen was indeed a Highlander.

The
Haunted
Hills

MONSAL DALE

'THE valley is gone and now every fool in Buxton can be in Bakewell in half an hour and every fool in Bakewell at Buxton, which you think a lucrative process of exchange you fools everywhere'.

SO WROTE John Ruskin over the controversial building of the railway viaduct in 1861. The artist John Ruskin felt very passionately about Monsal Dale for he described it as 'a rocky valley between Buxton and Bakewell, once upon a time as divine as the Vale of Tempe; you might have seen the gods there morning and evening – Apollo and all the sweet muses of light – walking in fair procession on the lawns of it, and to and fro among the pinnacles of its crags'.

Monsal Dale is undoubtedly one of the Peak District's busiest tourist attractions. The panoramic views across to the River Wye are unsurpassed. I must admit when I visited the district one could hardly imagine it to be haunted by demons, giants, tree spirits and water wraiths but my guide, a native of the area, assured me that local legend tells of Hob Hurst, who was traditionally a mischievous spirit of nature, being seen by visitors to the district.

Giants and demons were once believed to inhabit the dale, and today, when fierce winds blow, the howling sounds the wind creates would easily account for why people once believed this. The area also has a long history of being inhabited by witches, although there are no records of witches ever having been discovered practising their black arts in the area, there are still many rumours of mysterious hooded figures, carrying torches, and being seen in the dale late at night.

According to legend this valley is the haunt of devils, demons, giants and witches.

SOLDIER DICK

WHESTON HALL, a 17th-century building near Tideswell, once housed a life-size wooden figure of a Cromwellian soldier, which stood in the entrance hall. According to a local legend if the figure was ever removed from the hall then disaster would befall the occupants and the house. On several occasions the figure was removed from the house, normally whilst restorations were taking place, the ensuing chaos, crops failing, cattle dying, machinery continuously breaking down and the occupants falling ill, convinced the owners to reinstate the figure. Finally the figure was brought back to the hall and buried in the cellar where it is said to have remained. Since that day no more major misfortune has befallen the hall and as long as 'Soldier Dick', as he became known, stays buried at the hall all should continue to go well.

Other ghosts are reported to haunt the hall including an old lady who has made numerous appearances over the last century. At one time her appearances were so frequent that she lovingly became known as 'The Old Lady of Wheston Hall'. She is believed to be a former owner of the house who refuses to leave the building. A young woman with golden hair is also a frequently sighted spook. She is believed to be a lady who was originally from the village of Tideswell, who was coerced by her family to marry a man she did not love. Her intended love moved to Wheston Hall where he became a recluse. Stories soon began to emerge concerning black magic rituals being carried out at the hall. The husband of the lady concerned eventually vanished without a trace, it was later rumoured that the pair had murdered him and buried his body beneath an apple tree in the orchard. Soon after this event she moved into the hall and lived with her lover, this only reinforced the belief that her husband had befallen some foul deed. Several more years passed and eventually her lover died, some say claimed by the Devil. For the remainder of her life she stayed at Wheston Hall. After her death her ghost was seen to rise from its grave at Tideswell Church and visit the hall where she was seen to 'pass three times round the house'. Even in modern times her ghost has been seen wandering the grounds of the hall screeching whilst at the same time pulling at her long golden hair.

ARBOR LOW

ONE OF THE most ancient and sacred places in Derbyshire is Arbor Low, 'Stonehenge of the Peak'. The henge is over 1,230ft above sea level and although the stones now all lie flat to the ground it is still one of the most impressive and mysterious places in the Peak District. Arbor Low itself resembles a large clockface and the open views of the surrounding countryside and moors are breathtaking. From this elevated position one can see White Edge, Morridge and Stanage. One friend always describes the place as being like 'the top of the world' and, I must admit, that feeling does come to heart when you are standing there with the wind roaring, the skylarks flying around you and with the rolling clouds seeming so close to earth that you could reach up and touch them, it is easy to think back as if almost remembering a time long gone when our Pagan ancestors worshipped the elements and called on the power of the sun to give life.

Arbor Low is thought to have been a special place where priests and chieftains and important people may have been buried. The construction of the henge probably dates from 1700BC, and was certainly in use for many hundreds of years. Although excavations have been carried out in the vicinity and a complete human skeleton has been discovered in the centre of the henge suggesting that it may have been a human sacrifice, it seems extremely unlikely although this can not be proved.

Many books on magic and mysticism attribute stone circles as having strange powers, also that stone circles, pagan burial mounds, and other ancient sites have pathways of power that run between them called leys. Arbor Low is said to have as many as 50 of these leys that run through it and indeed lead from it, although Paul Devereux and Ian Thompson in their book, *The Ley Hunters Companion*, state that they were only able to find two which they would give credence to.

Then there are many writers that would try to ignore the very feeling of Arbor Low and testify that people can easily be duped into believing that places are haunted or have a feel-

Arbor Low (Stonehenge of the Peak). A magical place where many spirits are said to dwell.

ing of magic about them. Yes, while it may be possible for some people to be duped some of the time, we all know that people in general can not be so easily fooled all of the time. For centuries people have been experiencing strange occurrences and ghostly sightings at the stone circle as W. M. Turner demonstrates in his *Romances of the Peak*: 'Coming away from a visit there in 1897,

Arbor Low. Human remains found near to the centre of the stone circle when it was excavated in 1901.

I accosted a young herdsman, who was attending some cattle grazing by the wayside. After touching on several points I came cautiously to the Druidical circle business. I wanted to know how it came there and its purpose and so forth. He could not tell. It had been there undisturbed for generations and according to the account given him by the old people, and that was all, excepting, there may have been a battle there and people had been buried about the place. "How did he come to know that?" "Well you see", he said, "the folks round about never go that way at night for fear of boggarts. Several have been seen prowling about, and it is the common talk that people must have been buried there". "Did you ever go that way at night?" I asked. He said that he had not, but he bravely added, he would not mind, for he did not believe in such things.

ANAVIO

ORIGINALLY constructed of timber and turf the Roman fort of Anavio or Navio, at Brough in the High Peak, was rebuilt of gritstone in AD154 to 159 when the Roman soldiers were actively being attacked by Brigante warlords in open revolt of the Roman military suppression. The fort was built at an important river crossing where several significant trade routes crossed the Peak. Navio was linked with Buxton by Batham Gate, Melandra Castle (Ardotalia) by Doctors Gate, four miles south-east of Glossop, and Templeborough. All these Roman forts are believed to have had earth ramparts surmounted by a wooden stockade with a single ditch.

The perimeter walls of the fort were originally 20ft high and 7ft thick, extending to approximately 340ft by 285ft. As late as 1760 an inner building and several stone pillars were still said to be standing. In 1903 two altar stones were excavated, numerous archaeological finds may still be seen at Buxton Museum. Today all that remains of Anavio are a few stones in a field, a sad reminder of a once great empire which threatened to conquer and then rule the world.

Of the many Roman remains scattered throughout Derbyshire and the Peak District, there seems to be very few which are without their phantoms and spectres. Anavio however appears to have more than most, with ghosts that are said to appear in their hundreds. One local legend has it that on moonlit nights the haunting sound of a single horn being blown can be heard echoing throughout the valleys and the area immediately surrounding the Roman fort. Another legend tells of whole legions of Roman soldiers which have been spotted marching across the wind swept moors between Anavio and Melandra Castle at Glossop.

THE GHOSTS OF WIN HILL AND LOSE HILL

JUST NORTH of the village of Hope, not too far from Castleton, lie two hills known as Win Hill and Lose Hill. According to a local legend, over 1,300 years ago, a great battle took place within these hills, between Cuicholm, King of Wessex and Edwin, King of Northumbria. The story tells how Ceolwulf, King of Wessex, died in AD626 leaving his kingdom to be divided between his two sons, Cynegils and Cuicholm.

Before King Ceolwulf's death, King Edwin of Northumbria, knowing Ceolwulf was in a weakened condition, stole some of his land. Ceolwulf knew of Edwin's might and dared not take up the insult because he knew his armies were inferior. Cuicholm however, insulted by the theft of his father's land, planned a devious way to get back at King Edwin.

Cuicholm sent an envoy named Eumer, to see King Edwin. Once in the king's presence Eumer drew from his garments a double-edged dagger and lunged at King Edwin attempting to stab at his heart. Watching in the wings was a beautiful maidservant called Lilla who, realising that the king was about to be assassinated, threw herself in front of the blade of the assassin, the blade piercing her heart and Lilla falling dead at the king's feet, threw the court into a state of chaos.

The envoy was disarmed, a futile attempt was made to revive Lilla and the king immediately ordered that the would-be assassin be executed. Before Eumer died, from a torturous death, he confessed to the king that it was Cuicholm who

had sent him on his murderous mission. Immediately King Edwin summoned a council of war and began marching on Cuicholm.

Cuicholm having anticipated that there would be trouble, alerted his armies to be prepared to commence battle. Having an agreement with his brother Cynegils, that should he ever need him, then he would come, the two joined forces and began their march on Edwin. Penda, King of Mercia, being an old enemy of Edwin and jealous of his power joined forces with the two brothers in the hope of defeating Edwin.

Edwin's reputation for being a shrewd king was well known and had gained him a great deal of respect from his followers, Edwin was therefore determined not to disappoint his loyal followers. As the two armies approached each other Edwin decided that his best strategy would be to take up his battle stance on a nearby hill (Win Hill). Cuicholm and his armies arrived the following day and were disappointed to realise that

Lose Hill at Hope. A bloody battle is still said to be fought here at certain times of the year.

their only option was take over the next nearest hill (Lose Hill) and try to make the best of a bad situation.

The following morning ambassadors from both parties met on the banks of the River Noe, which happened to be placed strategically between the two hills. Both parties traded political insults threatening to destroy each other's armies and promising that the River Noe would run red with the blood of the defeated warriors. Shortly after the ambassadors had reported back to their kings the battle between the two armies commenced.

Before long the waters of the River Noe did indeed run red with the blood of warriors from each of the armies. Neither seemed to be winning but as the day drew on it appeared that the greater numbers of the Wessex army was at last beginning to defeat Edwin's. Edwin knew that all was not lost and at a strategic moment, when he knew that the battle was going against him, he gave a signal and his men began their retreat back up the hill. The men of Wessex took

their retreat as being a sign of defeat and, with a roar of victory, chased the fleeing warriors up the hill. Once the majority of Edwin's men were safely at the top of Win Hill they immediately set about throwing boulders and rocks, previously gathered the night before, down the hill, crushing most of the opposing Wessex warriors. Edwin, although he lost nearly half of his men, was pleased with his apparent win and returned to Northumbria satisfied that he had, at least in the greater part, taken revenge for the insult of the murder of Lilla and his attempted assassination.

It is said that from that day onward the two hills became known as Win Hill and Lose Hill, and although there is no historical evidence to support the story it is still accepted into local legend. As too are the stories of ghosts that haunt the two hills and I am told that on certain days and nights of the year a re-enactment of the savage battle between the two opposing forces can be heard; the clashing of swords, the cries of battle and the River Noe is still said to turn red with the ghostly blood of the long dead warriors.

STANTON MOOR

NOT TOO FAR AWAY from Birchover, in an elevated position above Darley Dale, is an ancient gritstone plateau known as Stanton Moor. Being about two miles in length and just over a mile in breadth, it is a strange and sometimes sinister place where few birds sing. The plateau is known to have been used between 2000 and 1500BC. Most of the archaeological finds date from this era. Probably used as a religious gathering place and burial grounds, there is much speculation as to the original purpose for ancient man's fascination with the plateau. The barrows were excavated under the direction of two local archaeologists, J.C.Heathcote and his

son J.P.Heathcote. The Bronze Age peoples who inhabited the vicinity were known to cremate their dead. Many of the burial mounds excavated contained cinerary urns, flint tools and a selection of jewellery, these finds were discovered at the edge of the moor in one of the smaller stone circles.

Many modern day witches still gather on Stanton Moor to celebrate their four great Sabbaths and four lesser Esbats throughout the pagan year. I am told by several witches that the moor can sometimes have a menacing feeling. Many witches feel that the moor has become corrupted by evil and sinister practises over the centuries. This feeling of evil is apparently more evident

The Nine Ladies Stone Circle on Stanton Moor. Suicide victims, murderers and witches were once buried on or near the moor in a bid to stop their spirits from walking.

around what is undoubtedly Stanton Moor's most famous feature, the Nine Ladies stone circle.

The stone circle is 35ft in diameter and surrounded by a shallow mound. To the south-west of the circle is the 'King Stone' or as some people call it the 'Fiddler's Chair'. According to legend it was here that the Devil played his fiddle to nine dancing ladies on the Sabbath. So infuriated was God, at their outright disregard for his holy day, that he turned the dancers into stone, there to remain as a reminder to all those who would thwart the commands of the lord. There are many reports of people who have actually experienced strange occurrences on the

moor including one lady who informed me that she had been abducted by a UFO.

Strange lights have been seen on the moor, as has the ghost of a white lady. The Earl Grey Monument, located at the edge of the moor, is said to be the haunt of a spectral black dog with huge flaming eyes, a foaming mouth and huge teeth.

A reference in Youlgreave Parish Church records recalls an incident in 1779 when men were paid money for carrying corpses to Stanton Moor, 'To Ale and bread and cheese to ye men that went with the corpses. For ceredge of the corpses on to Stanton Moor'. This incident was probably for the burial of a suicide, murderer or suspected witch, as this was the custom of that time. Crossroads were believed to harbour the spirits of those that were buried there. A suggestion as to why suspected witches and such were buried in this way is offered in Elliot O'Donnell's book *Haunted Britain* (1948):

'Some think it is because in olden times murderers, sorcerers and suicides were buried at crossroads, with a stake thrust through them in a foolishly vain attempt to keep their spirits from wandering; others think it because witches and wizards were believed to hold orgies and practise the black art at crossroads while others, again, think crossroads, like lonely pools, old quarries and some woods, have a peculiar attraction for a certain species of spirit.'

THE GHOST OF LOST LAD

THERE are several stories concerning the ghostly legend of the Lost Lad. The following is perhaps one of the more better known versions of the story. The tale concerns a young teenage boy, named Abraham, who lived in the 16th century in the village of Derwent with his mother. The village has since been submerged beneath the waters of the Ladybower Reservoir. Abraham's father had died when he was very young, leaving Abraham alone with his poor mother to care for and run a small farm. As the years passed by Abraham, who had grown into a strong young man, would gain great pleasure from looking after the farm and tending his animals. The work that Abraham favoured most on the farm was looking after the sheep, for he loved nothing better than to wander the lonely hills with his flock deep within his own thoughts. One particularly cold and harsh winter the snow fell so thickly that the village became cut off from the outside world.

For several days the snow fell continuously and Abraham became increasingly worried about his beloved animals who had been left to fend for themselves. Finally the snow stopped falling and the weather cleared enough for people to come out of their houses again. Abraham's mother sent the boy to look for the sheep on the hills, instructing him to bring them back to the farm before nightfall. With a cheerful wave the boy set off to look for the sheep with his faithful dog by his side. Heading for Derwent Edge Abraham climbed the steep hills and before long managed to locate several of his sheep. So engrossed was he that he did not notice that the weather had began to rapidly deteriorate. Before long it had began to snow heavily and a thick mist swept through the valleys, obliterating the familiar landmarks.

Abraham wandered for several hours becoming increasingly lost in a blizzard that had now began to rage. Finally Abraham realised that he had to find shelter from the severe cold and biting winds, so, finding a rock large enough for him to crawl beneath, Abraham took shelter from the elements and squeezed himself into a rock crevice hoping that the blizzard would soon abate and allow him to continue his task. Alas, the bad weather continued and before long Abraham was fighting himself not to fall asleep, in a last effort to occupy himself he managed to find a sharp stone and scratch the words 'LOST LAD' on to it. Frozen and hungry Abraham's strength finally left him and he fell into a deep cold sleep, a sleep which he was never to rouse from. The boy's sheepdog, which had faithfully continued to remain by his side, also finally succumbed to the bitter conditions and died.

Back at the farm Abraham's mother waited and watched the landscape from her window for any sign of the boy, no sign of him was forthcoming. 'The Parnassus of the Peak', Richard

Back Tor, near the Ladybower Reservoir. The ghosts of a young boy and his faithful dog are often seen wandering the lonely hills.

Furness, in his poem *A Tale of Derwent*, explains how:

> 'Ere this his mother, o'er the
>   moorland hill,
> Foreboded Abraham lost, or many an
>   ill,
> As anxiously, or ere the clock struck
>   four,
> She gazed till her eyes could gaze no more,
> "He comes not still!" she said, "tis dark no
>   moon!
> Oh! woe betide me, if comes not soon.
> Why did I let him Go?"

The next day a search party was organised and the boy's mother, accompanied by most of the villagers, set out on to the snow covered hills to look for any signs of the boy. They searched all day but the blizzard had covered any tracks the boy had left. Eventually night fell and the search had to be called off only to resume the following morning which still proved futile. Finally tired and saddened by what they now knew was his fate the villagers gave up their search and abandoned any hope of ever finding him.

Eventually winter gave way to spring and the shepherds returned to the hills to tend their sheep. One shepherd, walking in the region of Back Tor, passed a stone where he spied the words 'LOST LAD' scratched upon it. His curiosity roused, the shepherd investigated further and found the remains of Abraham and his faithful dog beneath. Gathering several large stones the shepherd made a marker so as to recognise the place again. From that day, and it is said for at least 100 years after, passing shepherds would place a stone on the spot until eventually a large cairn was created which can still be seen today.

It is still believed that whenever there is going to be a particularly bad winter the ghost of Abraham and his faithful dog can be seen wandering the moors and hills of Back Tor, a warning to would be travellers to turn back lest they too meet with a terrible death. Farmers have been known to take heed of the appearance of Abraham and one farmer, who I will call Jack, told me that he had seen the boy and dog high in the hills, and, knowing their significance, brought his animals nearer to his farm. Sure enough, the very next day, the snows began to fall and the ensuing winter was one of the worst that Jack could remember.

HAUNTED CAVES AND CAVERNS

THERE ARE very few caves and caverns in Derbyshire and the Peak District which have not, at some point in time, been purported to have been haunted or associated with supernatural creatures. Poole's Cavern, originally one of the 'Seven Wonders of the Peak', has long been associated with ghosts and strange occurrences. Poole was said to have been an outlaw who used the cavern as a storehouse for his stolen loot sometime around the year 1440, during the reign of Henry VI. Local legend still tells the story that much of the loot has never been found, and that the greedy ghost of the outlaw, Poole, still guards the treasure which is hidden deep within the cave. Poole's Cavern was also known to have been used by our ancient forefathers who used the cave as a place of shelter and worship. Archaeological excavations inside the cavern have uncovered several hundred examples of Roman bronze brooches, many in the form of seahorses and dolphins suggesting that part of the cavern was once used as a shrine to subterranean water gods and sprites during Roman occupation. Sculls, bones, and pottery dating from a much earlier age, have also been uncovered inside the cave and nearby, at the prehistoric burial mound Grin Low, there is evidence to suggests that the whole area was once used as a burial ground which may account for the many strange stories of ghosts and spectres that are believed to haunt the area.

Many caves and caverns were believed to be associated with the Devil. Several were thought to be frequented by witches and devil worshippers, as in the case of many of the caves in the Matlock area. One in particular, I am informed, is still used by practising witches. Derbyshire's alleged oldest witchcraft coven, 'The Coven of the Ram', is still said to practice their ancient religion in one of the caves around Matlock Bath, another cave in this area is said to be haunted by a whole battalion of Roman soldiers, while one of the petrifying wells at Matlock Bath, which used to attract several thousand visitors a year, is home to a water sprite and an apparition of an old lady in a shawl.

Peak Cavern at Castleton was at one time occupied by rope makers. These subterranean workers were allowed to live there rent free, as they specialised in the making of hangmens' ropes and nooses. No one had the courage to ask the ropemakers, who lived in two cottages just within the mouth of the entrance to the cavern, for money, for fear of being cursed by them, for many locals believed that if they crossed or slighted the rope makers in any way then they would end up dangling from the end of one of their ropes. The Devil himself was said to visit Peak Cavern on certain nights of the year, and locally the cave became known as 'The Devil's Arse', after heavy rains the water from the surroundings moors seeped down through the hills and poured out of the mouth of the cave this was said to vaguely resemble Satan relieving himself. The cave, which is a natural cave unlike many in the area, is also said to be haunted by an old man thought to be one of the previous rope makers whose life was ended in a terrible accident there.

Another famous haunted cave is Eldon Hole at Peak Forest, between Castleton and Buxton. Eldon Hole takes its name from 'Elves Hill' as too does Eldon Hill, an ancient burial mound nearby. Known as another of the 'Seven Wonders of the Peak', Eldon Hole was in ancient times feared as being haunted by demons, as locals believed it to be bottomless and therefore they felt it inevitably lead directly to hell. In the early part of the 18th century Daniel Defoe told of a rope being lowered nearly a mile into the hole, but it is now known to be only 245ft deep. Also recorded was the alleged murder of a traveller who was forced to walk over the edge, by two particularly nasty villains, until he 'stept at once into eternity'. In the 16th century the Earl of Leicester is said to have lowered a local down into the hole to ascertain its true depth but, when the poor fellow was hauled back out of the hole, he had gone crazy and shortly afterwards died. The Earl concluded that he must have come face to face with the Devil himself. Shortly after this event the hole became known locally as the 'Devil's Bolt Hole'. Eldon Hole was first explored in 1780 and revealed a huge domed cavern, its roof encrusted by masses of stalactites, it is now occasionally used by potholers.

Many of the old lead mines throughout the Peak District are known to be haunted. Most of them are rumoured to be haunted by long dead miners brassbound on never giving up their right to the rich ore that lies beneath the green hills of the Peak. Miners were well known to have been superstitious peoples, a clue being in some of the names they called their mines, God-be-here, Daily Bread, Chance, Venture and Good Luck Mine etc. It is estimated that at, least 100,000 shafts are scattered throughout the Peak, many being shallow and blocked and even more being deep and dangerous. Much has been written concerning ghosts that haunt the mines of the Peak, my favourite being a poem by Mr Henry Walker, who was said to be a keen observer of local folklore and traditions. The following is one of his Peakland poems which captures the essence of haunted mines.

> From flickering tallow candle the lead miner
>   flicks the 'thief',
> To rid the 'spirit' splutter in his quaint and
>   crude belief.
> Then, turning quickly, down the vein he
>   sees a pale light shine.
> His heart beats fast. Is it the
> Spectre of the Mine?
>
> Along the silent gallery and gripping his
>   candle tight,
> Swiftly the miner followed, but as swiftly
>   sped the light,
> Till, at the limit of the vein, it vanished
>   without sign.
> The miner's blood ran cold. It was the
> Spectre of the Mine.
>
> A sudden crash and fall of rocks. The miner
>   met his doom,
> And shining ore he vainly sought now
>   glistened on his tomb.
> In lead miners lore 'tis written, let those
>   who can define
> Why none may live that look upon the
>   Spectre of the Mine.

According to an article in the *Derbyshire Countryside* magazine of 1957, one such 'Spectre of the Mine' was photographed by a group of speleologists at the Magpie Mine, near Sheldon. The writer, Mr R.A.H.O'Neil, wrote the following concerning the alleged incident: 'Several mines were said to be haunted and one, the Magpie Mine, near Bakewell, has recently produced some evidence that it is. Just after the war a party of speleologists were exploring the mine when one of them reported that he had seen a man with a candle walking along the tunnel from which he had disappeared without trace. A photograph of another member of the party on a raft in a sough at the mine showed a second man standing, apparently, on 9ft of water. The old man was clearly either trying to protect his ancient rights or to help the 20th century searchers find the ore, which is reported to be thick and pure in the main vein now 150 feet below the water level.'

Another type of ghost that haunts many a mine is the 'Ghost Dog', which nearly always seems to be an omen of bad luck. One story tells of a miner from Bradwell, near Castleton, who came across a huge phantom black dog on his way home one moonlit night. Another ghostly dog haunts the Odin Mine at Castleton, which, according to legend, was worked as a penal settlement under the invading Norsemen, who are thought to have named the mine after there mythological giver of victory. Men, women, and children, worked as much as 800 tons of lead ore annually and although sections of the mine are still accessible to cavers its main interest for anyone visiting the area will be the crushing circle which still survives just above the Treak Cliff Cavern.

A more terrifying ghost dog is said to haunt one of the caves at Matlock Bath and has also been seen wandering amongst the hills in the area. The dog is said to be of a huge size, have large staring eyes and ferocious looking long

Thor's Cave. A notoriously haunted cave which has been named after the Norse Thunder God.

yellow teeth. Yet another ghost dog, this time accompanied by an old man in a hat and long coat, has been seen at Sallet Hole Mine near Stoney Middleton, who, when approached, vanishes into thin air. Another vanishing ghost has been seen, on several occasions, at the Cotgrave Pit near Chesterfield. Appearing in a more modern day apparel he is said to walk through walls causing much distress to those who have encountered him. So distressed was one miner that he flatly refused to ever work down that mine again.

Strange voices and knocking noises have often been reported by miners who work in the depths of the earth. One such mine was near Eyam where a miner, busy working in his mine one day, heard a voice, as if from deep within the earth call out "Go on, there's ore. Go on there's ore". Thinking that it must be a message from some unseen presence, the miner searched for many months but found not a trace of a vein of lead anywhere. Eventually becoming disillus-

ioned he gave up his search and sold the deed of the mine to another miner. Before long news spread that the new owner of the mine had found a rich vein of lead ore, deep within the mine, which was to make him a very wealthy man, proving that the disembodied ghostly voice was after all correct.

Other omens of doom in mining folklore included 'the Fiery Drake', said to be a strange spherical flame which would often appear prior to a disaster, although in many parts of the Derbyshire it was considered, when it appeared, to indicate where there was a rich vein of lead ore.

When I visited the Blue John Mine at Castleton I was informed by the gentleman leading the tour that the mine was believed to have numerous ghosts. One ghost in particular would always let you know of his presence by a ghostly whistle which could be heard coming along the tunnels towards you, when it seemed that the person whistling was nearly upon you it would suddenly stop, further investigations in the mine

The Blue John Mine, Castleton. A whistling ghost and a 'Grey Man' are two spirits which haunt this famous mine.

would reveal no other presence. Also said to haunt the Blue John Mine is a man who has been spotted on numerous occasions wearing a plain grey outfit, this phantom also vanishes as the individual approaches.

At Cresswell Crags, close to the Nottinghamshire border, there have been uncovered many remains of Palaeolithic man which are thought to be some of the most important finds of earliest man to be discovered of recent times. The caves naturally carved within the cliffs have produced some remarkable finds including the remains of mammoth bones and several artistically carved bones which are of massive historical interest. Ghosts are said to be numerous here, of recent times there have been several appearances of a

phantom cave man, dressed in furs and skins he has been seen standing in the entrance of several caves.

Perhaps the most curious cave in the Peak District is that of Thor's Cave, located within the scenic Manifold Valley. Situated high above the valley and not too far from Wetton Village, this natural antediluvian cave is thought to have sheltered man since earliest times. The name is thought to derive from Thor, the Norse God of Thunder, who was the son of the God Woden. The cave was first seriously excavated in 1864-65 by the Midland Scientific Association under the direction of Samuel Carrington of Wetton. The cave revealed many interesting finds including, flint arrowheads, an iron adze,

The Peak Cavern at Castleton. At one time this distinctive cave was named after a piece of the Devil's anatomy, as dark muddy waters running from the local hills were said to resemble the Devil relieving himself.

bronze brooches indicating that the cave was actively used from the Romano-British to the present times. A human skeleton was excavated from the site and was found to have originally been placed in its final resting place in an upright position. The skeleton is thought to date from the Neolithic age.

There are several other caves in the locality and they too have said to have been haunted at some time or another. The most frequently sighted spook in the area is that of a Roman soldier who has been seen standing just inside the entrance to Thor's Cave. Also in abundance are tales of a green man seen wandering through the woods. Thor's Cave was once believed to be one of the many homes of Hob O'th Hurst, or as locals in the area called him 'Fiddling Hob'. When the wind blows through the valley and passes the entrance of the cave, the resulting sound is said to be reminiscent of a violin being played badly. This spooky noise led to the belief that it was the spirit of Hob screeching to be fed, many locals would not pass near the cave once night had fallen.

Thor's Cave has also featured of recent times in the horror cult classic film, *Lair of the White Worm*, when it was portrayed as the home of a giant snake. It is not hard to see why this dramatic cave was chosen for the film, nor is it hard to understand why ancient man regarded the cave as an entrance to another supernatural world. According to a local legend there is a secret entrance to Fairyland somewhere at the back of the cave, the only catch is that in order to find the entrance you must first have the gift of second sight.

HARBOROUGH ROCKS

OCATED not too far from Brassington, Harborough Rocks have long had an association with Druids. Many of the rocks at this site are carved into curious shapes. Some people maintain that it was once an evil place where witches and devil worshippers gathered to hold high jubilee and plan what evil deeds they would do next.

As to who carved the stones, no one seems to know, but it is thought that a local man may have been responsible several centuries ago. One curious feature of Harborough Rocks was that it was once the scene of a haunted rocking stone which would move from side to side by itself, even when there was no wind. Another similar stone once existed at Rowter Rocks, another site said to be the haunt of malevolent spooks, but the stone was toppled by a group of boys in the 18th century.

Other ghosts are said to haunt the site including strange wispy lights that are seen floating about the rocks late at night. Other people maintain that the ghost of a man, not unlike a Roman soldier can also be seen at the site.

Several other strangely carved rocks include a giant's chair, a pulpit and a font. Some rocks and stones are said to resemble faces, especially in the late autumn when the natural light of evening casts shadows at a certain angle.

Harborough Rocks at Brassington. A haunted rocking stone that moved by itself even when there was no wind once existed at the rocks.

Whispering Dead

EYAM

HE BEAUTIFUL quaint village of Eyam is perhaps best remembered for its plague victims. The plague was brought to the village in 1665 in a consignment of clothes from London, five out of every six people died within just a few months. Writing in the 1920s H.V.Morton wrote 'In the quiet Derbyshire village of Eyam, men still talk about the Plague of London as though it happened last week'. The situation is much the same today and thousands of people still visit the village each year to see the scene of the terrible yet famous tragedy.

The dead were buried at several sites around the village in hastily-constructed graves. Services were conducted by the Reverend William Mompesson, who took to preaching in a dell not too far from the village from a tall stone, to this day the dell is known as 'Cucklet Church'. An annual commemoration service is held at the dell on the last Sunday in August.

William Mompesson managed to rally the people together, giving them hope and inevitably he managed to stop the plague from spreading to other villages. His wife, Catherine Mompesson, died at the height of the outbreak, her ghost is said to haunt the churchyard of St Lawrence, where she is seen to wander between the church and the rectory, hesitating momentarily at the Great Eyam Cross. The late Clarence Daniel, author of two books on Derbyshire ghosts, and a local historian of Eyam wrote how he 'had been assured by a parishioner that occupants of the rectory had heard the whisper of ghostly gowns and had actually seen Mrs Catherine Mompesson who died there during the plague of 1665-6. The rector told me that mysterious happenings had occurred. Sometimes, when entertaining guests, he and his wife had been asked whether someone had been ill in the night, because the visitors had heard footsteps passing along the corridor, and doors being opened and closed… A former maid at the rectory met, as she supposed, Mrs Mompesson ascending the back stairs, and described her as wearing a large hat.'

Eyam Hall, built in 1676 and lived in by the Wright family, was once the haunt

(Top): Eyam Hall. Previous owners of the hall were so troubled by a ghost of an old man that they kept a bedroom door permanently locked. (Bottom) The Great Cross of Eyam. The ghost of Catherine Mompesson, a victim of the plague, is seen to hesitate at the cross momentarily, then pass into the church.

Plague Cottages, Eyam. The plague was first introduced to the village in a bundle of clothes delivered to one of these cottages.

of an old man who frequented a room upstairs. So regular was the appearance of his ghost in the room that the then owners took to keeping the door locked.

The 'Plague Cottages', as they have become known, where the first victim of the plague is said to have perished, are notoriously haunted. One former resident refused to sleep in one of the bedrooms as he was consistently disturbed from his sleep to find the ghost of a woman in a plain blue smock. He later described the lady as being a 'pleasant faced lady', who simply stood and watched him before fading away.

SACRED TO THE MEMORY OF THE HANCOCK FAMILY VICTIMS OF THE PLAGUE AUGUST 3RD - 10TH 1666

VISITORS ARE REQUESTED TO TREAT THIS BURIAL PLACE WITH REVERENCE

Other sites around the village are also said to be haunted, Mompesson's Well, where food was once left by outsiders during the plague, is haunted by a small boy who has been seen standing close to the site. The Riley Graves, situated on a hillside just outside the village, is the haunt of a blue lady. People walking to the stone-walled encircled site have seen the blue lady from a distance and she appears to be attending the graves. When they get up close to the site they find no one there but themselves.

Eyam Dale is the scene of a strange haunting by a 'phantom cyclist', who has been spotted by numerous locals, late at night at Top Scrin, near the top of the dale. The ghost was once spotted in the pouring rain peddling at a fast pace. Although the rain was falling in torrents the cyclist

The Riley Graves. The ghost of an old lady has been seen tending these plague graves.

appeared to be completely dry. Other phantom bicycle riders have been reported in Derbyshire, one at Long Lane near Thurvaston and the other at Blagreaves Lane, in the Derby suburb of Littleover.

Many other reports abound of ghosts at Eyam village, to mention them all would perhaps be a little laborious, but it can generally be accepted that Eyam is undoubtedly one of, if not the most haunted village in Derbyshire and the Peak District.

MARY, QUEEN OF SCOTS

OF THE MANY tragic stories concerning prominent figures in history, few stories can compare with the ill-fated Mary, Queen of Scots. Nearly all of the many places where Mary was held captive, are said to be haunted by her unhappy ghost. She is undoubtedly Derbyshire's most prolific ghost, perhaps the injustices she suffered keeps her spirit walking the earth, or perhaps the appearance of her ghost is just a type of recording, as it seems rather odd

that she should simultaneously haunt so many buildings. However, her ghost will continue to be Derbyshire's most tragic historical phantom.

Mary was born at the Palace of Linlithgow on 8 December 1542, the news of her birth was carried to her father, James V of Scotland, as he lay dying. The King had been defeated in the Battle of Solway Moss, and in a state of depression and illness had retired to Falkland Palace. While at the palace he was given the news that his French wife, Mary of Guise, had

The tragic figure of Mary, Queen of Scots is reputed to haunt nearly all the buildings in which she was once held prisoner.

given birth to a daughter, upon which he is reputed to have muttered "The de'il go wi' it." In less than a week the King was dead and the "puir wee lass", as he called her on his death bed, became the Queen of Scotland.

Almost immediately negotiations commenced concerning who she should marry. The English, being eager to put an end to the hostilities which lay between them and Scotland, attempted to match Prince Edward, the son of King Henry VIII, this was eventually agreed by the Treaties of Greenwich. When Catherine de Medici, wife of King Henry, the future King of France, gave birth to a boy in 1544, new plans were drawn up, and a match with France was now considered more favourable.

When Henry VIII realised what had happened he became furious, and immediately began his 'Rough Wooing', his armies were dispatched to make constant attacks on Scotland. In order to protect Mary, she was moved about to several different locations, eventually she was sent to Inchmahome Priory on an island in the Trossachs, until it was deemed safe for her to return.

In 1547 King Henry II of France offered his son, Francis as a bridegroom, and several months later a contract was drawn up, one of the conditions stipulated was that, when necessary, the French would provide armies for Scotland when they were needed.

When Queen Mary was five years old she was taken to France, there she was to remain for the next 13 years. Much of her time in France was spent being educated at the sophisticated French Court. She became fluent in several languages, her favourite being French, which she spoke and wrote excellently for the rest of her life.

On 24 April 1558, Queen Mary married Prince Francis amidst much pomp and splendour, in the Cathedral of Notre Dame. It is extremely doubtful that the marriage was ever consummated, historians tend to agree that Francis was incapable of ever fathering a child.

In November of the same year Queen Elizabeth ascended the throne of England, amidst much controversy. When King Henry VIII was divorced from Catherine of Aragon, it was never accepted by the Catholic Church. This meant that King Henry VIII's marriage to Elizabeth's mother, Ann Boleyn, was, to the Catholics, void as his divorce had never been, nor ever would be, granted. Therefore Elizabeth, to the Catholics, was illegitimate and Queen Mary, as a great-granddaughter to Henry VII was the rightful Queen of England. King Henry of France immediately let it be known that Mary was the rightful heir and proclaimed her as Queen of England, Scotland and Ireland. Queen Elizabeth was said to have been furious.

In the following year King Henry died when he was severely wounded in a jousting contest, and Mary and Francis became the new King and Queen of France. In 1560, after much suffering, Francis died from an ear infection which went to his brain. Soon afterwards, Queen Mary decided to return to Scotland, which had undergone a great deal of political and religious change whilst she was away. Arriving at Leigh, then embarking for Holyrood, she was greeted warmly by the people wherever she went.

On 29 July 1565, at Holyrood, Queen Mary married Lord Henry Darnley, son of the Earl and

Wingfield Manor. One of the many buildings which Mary, Queen of Scots is said to haunt. This tower is where Mary was kept prisoner whilst at Wingfield.

Countess of Lennox, and a favourite of Queen Elizabeth. Lord Darnley, over 6ft tall and, unsure of his sexual preferences, was known to indulge in unnatural practices. Mary was initially so infatuated with him that she could see no faults. By the time she fell pregnant the Queen had become acquainted with, and grown close to, an Italian named David Riccio, whom she appointed her personal secretary. Queen Mary had grown tired of Darnley, his debaucheries, his pompous attitude, so much so that a rift grew between the two and, when in each other's company, they would openly bicker.

Darnley, full of malice at having been continuously spurned by the Queen, who spent a great deal of her spare time with Riccio, hatched a plan to get his own back. One evening whilst Mary was in her chambers, talking with Riccio, Darnley burst in and with several accomplices dragged Riccio outside, where they brutally stabbed him to death.

Not too long after this event at Edinburgh Castle, Queen Mary gave birth to a son whom she called James, later he was to become King James I of England and James VI of Scotland. When the child was presented to Darnley, Queen Mary is reputed to have said "gotten by none but you", for years afterwards rumours

were to circulate that the child was no other than Riccio's.

Mary having never forgiven her husband for the murder of Riccio, is believed to have conspired, to murder him. On 9 February 1567, Darnley who was recovering from the pox, was staying at a house in Kirk O'Field, when in the early hours of the morning it was blown to pieces with gunpowder. When his body was recovered, and later examined, it was discovered that he had in fact died of strangulation. The Earl of Bothwell was charged and brought to trial where he was later acquitted. Queen Elizabeth was said to be furious, she called the trial a travesty, sarcastically adding that Queen Mary must have been 'looking through her fingers'.

On 15 May 1567 Queen Mary married Bothwell at Holyrood amidst a great deal of scandal. Many people were now convinced that Mary had indeed been involved in the death of Lord Darnley, Knox publicly denounced Mary as a 'Scottish whore'. The nobles took up arms and on 15 June Queen Mary was

The Raised Summer House at Chatsworth. Known also as 'Queen Mary's Bower', her ghost is reputed to be seen walking down these stone steps.

taken prisoner at Carberry Hill. Later she was moved to the island of Lochleven, here she had a miscarriage which revealed she had been carrying twins. Being in a weakened state, and desperately unhappy, she was constantly pressured by Moray, to sign a deed of abdication in favour of her son James, this she eventually agreed to do and the child was crowned King at Stirling on 29 July 1567.

A plot was hatched by George Douglas, brother to the Lord of Lochleven, who arranged for Mary to escape from the island whilst a May Day celebration was taking place. Having successfully made her escape, she headed for Hamilton where she was warmly received by the people. Over 6,000 supporters flocked to the aid of Queen Mary and on 12 May 1567, her army was defeated.

Over the next two years a great deal of unhappiness ensued for Queen Mary, she was constantly moved, from place to place in a bid to stop her from being rescued. Several plots were contrived to secure her release but none of them were successful. Queen Elizabeth refused to help her, declaring that she could do little until her innocence in the matter of the murder of Lord Darnley had been clarified.

In 1569 George Talbot, 6th Earl of Shrewsbury, was given custody of Queen Mary. He was to remain her captor until 1584. It was about this time that Anthony Babington arrived firmly on the scene. Anthony was a handsome man who, at the age of ten had been made a ward of the 6th Earl of Shrewsbury, fourth husband of Bess of Hardwick. Babington became a page to Mary and soon became infatuated with her. Like her, he was a devout Catholic and believed that she was the rightful Queen of England.

In a bid to bring this about, Babington plotted with other Catholic conspirators and invited King Philip II of Spain to send an army to invade England – as he eventually attempted in 1588 when the Armada foundered. Babington planned

to murder Queen Elizabeth and put Mary, Queen of Scots on the throne of England. Tragically for the conspirators, Sir Francis Walsingham, Elizabeth's 'spy catcher', uncovered the plot after intercepting letters between Babington and Mary, which were sent from various places such as Tutbury Castle and Chartley Manor via a Burton Brewer who smuggled the letters in a watertight barrel.

Using the information from the so called Babington Plot, Walsingham gathered enough information to have Mary, Queen of Scots tried for treason and condemned to death. On the night of 13 January 1585, Mary's coach had trundled across little St Mary's Bridge, the only bridge over the River Derwent into Derby, taking her up St Peter's Street to the home of Sir Anthony Babington. Mary was being taken from Wingfield Manor to Tutbury Castle and she spent her last night in Derbyshire in Babington Hall – ironically, in the home of the man whose desire to see her as Queen of England would end in her execution.

Later that year, Babington, John Ballard (a Catholic priest of Rheims and Babington's main conspirator) and five other men were tried before a special commission. Babington attempted to lay the blame on Ballard and wrote to Queen Elizabeth beseeching her to work a miracle of mercy upon him and spare his life. To a friend he promised the sum of £1,000 if his release could be obtained. This was to no avail and on 20 September 1585, Babington, Ballard, and their five co-conspirators were taken to St Giles's in London where they were hanged, drawn and quartered. Anthony Babington declared from the scaffold that no private ends had influenced him and he believed his part in the plot to be 'a deed lawful and meritorious'. Mary was executed 17 months later at Fotheringhay Castle in Northamptonshire on 8 February 1587. Her body was first buried in Peterborough Cathedral but when her son ascended the English throne as James I, he had it removed to Westminster Abbey where it lies today beneath a magnificent white marble monument.

Shortly after Mary had been beheaded in the Great Hall of Fotheringhay Castle – the executioner Simon Bull apparently took three blows to sever her head with an axe – rumours began to circulate that her ghost had been seen wandering through several of the houses, manors and castles in which she had been imprisoned. Many of the houses in Derbyshire and Staffordshire still hold firm to the belief that her ghost walks the corridors and halls.

At Chatsworth House there is a raised summer house which is known to be one of the places where Mary, Queen of Scots was imprisoned. It is here, as well as at Tutbury Castle, Buxton, Wingfield Manor and the site where Babington House in Derby once stood on Babington Lane, that the ghost of the ill-fated Queen has been seen. The raised summer house at Chatsworth known as Queen Mary's Bower which bears her coat of arms above the iron gateway at the top of the stairs, is also a haunt for her unhappy spirit.

Sir Anthony Babington, it is said frequently stole into Wingfield Manor to see Mary, who was held in the tower there. Legend says that he used to disguise himself by rubbing the oil of walnuts on to his skin, which stained the flesh, giving him the appearance of someone much older. One particular night, while sneaking passed the guards, Babington was disturbed by a soldier and, in his haste to get out of sight, dropped from his pocket a walnut, which over a period of time seeded itself and grew into a great walnut tree which may still be seen within the ruins today.

The ghosts of the would-be lovers still haunt the grounds of the manor, there being several people, including one couple, who swear that they have encountered the two walking in the grounds. The iron bars and guards that may have kept them apart while flesh clung to their bones has no power to do the same in death. At Chatsworth House Mary's ghost is seen ascending the steps of her bower and, according to a gardener I spoke with, she walks about the area immediately in front of the raised summer house, she then walks back up the steps before vanishing.

HAUNTED MILLS

TODAY THERE are very few remains of the once common site of mills that scattered the face of the countryside. They were normally located by running water, which provided a power source although later it was found that the power being produced was not enough, and it was soon found necessary to install steam engines to pump water for the water wheel or as the main power source. Cotton spinning mills, many under licence from Arkwright, were erected at Bamford, Mayfield, Measham, Lumsdale, Borrowash, Lea and Wilne, all between 1780 and 1820.

Derbyshire was once a thriving industry for cotton mills. The labour force for the mills usually came from the locality, although more remote mills such as Litton and Mellor recruited pauper workers from anywhere in Britain.

Several accounts exist concerning the harsh conditions which many of the child workers are said to have endured. Perhaps the most famous of these accounts is by Robert Blincoe who was placed in St Pancras Workhouse in 1796, at the age of four and later spent time in many cotton mills including Litton. The following is a short extract from an official report which Blincoe helped develop, the report still resides within the Parliamentary papers of 1833:

'I have seen the time when two hand-vices of

a pound weight each, more or less, have been screwed to my ears, at Litton Mill in Derbyshire. These are the scars still remaining behind my ears. Then three or four of us have been hung at once on a cross-beam above the machinery, hanging by our hands, without shirts or stockings. Then we used to stand up, in a skip, without our shirts, and be beaten with straps or sticks; the skip was to prevent us from running away from the straps. Then they used to tie up a 28 pounds weight, one or two at once, according to our size, to hang down our backs, with no shirt on.'

The claims of Robert Blincoe have been denounced by many historians as exaggerated, whilst this may be partly true, it is also recognised that children did indeed suffer harsh, often sadistic, sufferings under the hand of mill owners who were responsible for the children's health and safety.

Arkwright's Mill at Cromford. Many such mills are said to be the haunt of children who worked there.

There appear to be few mills in Derbyshire that are not haunted, in some way, or another, by the ghosts of the children who once worked there. Many claims of children having died at such mills exist, although there is little documented evidence to suggest that the numbers of children who perished at these mills were any greater than the natural mortality figures of England as a whole. Litton Mill is renowned for being haunted by several spirit children, as too is Arkwright's Mill at Cromford, which, apart from being the haunt of Sir Richard Arkwright himself, it is also the haunt of a gentleman dressed in a uniform not unlike the fashion of a policeman of earlier times.

FAIR FLORA

STANDING on a hillside above the River Derwent, near Grindleford, is Stoke Hall built in 1755 for Lord Bradford. The hall has always had a reputation for being haunted by numerous spirits. The main ghost is said to be that of 'Fair Flora', a statue that once stood near the hall. There are so many versions of the ghost stories concerning the ghosts of the hall, that it is extremely difficult to differentiate which version might be closer to the factual or historical truth. The statue, which the stories evolve around, is believed to have originated from Chatsworth House. R.Murray Gilchrist describing the hall mentions how: 'Farther down the valley a strange 18th-century house stands on a thickly wooded bank of the river. This is Stoke Hall, once the Peakland home of the Earls of Bradford. The neighbouring folk in former years used to tell a weird story of a skull that haunted the upper story, and one may be sure that they feared to pass alone after 'edge o' dark'. Although Stoke has no pretensions to architectural beauty, its position suggests romance and mystery. In the wood nearby stands a renaissance statue known as 'Fair Flora', a gift of the 'long-armed' Duke of

Devonshire to a member of the Bridgeman family, but by popular belief a monument raised to the memory of a young lady who was murdered by a jealous lover.'

Other ghosts are said to haunt the hall including, a maid servant who was murdered in the upper rooms of the house, indelible blood stains in several of the rooms, a headless lady seen walking down the stairs, phantom footsteps, strange whispering and rustling sounds and a weeping spirit which can only be heard on certain nights of the year.

Clarence Daniel in his book *Haunted Derbyshire* (1975) describes how he was once told how: 'the statue had been given to a Mrs Taylor who had admired it when visiting Chatsworth. But with the statue came a spell of misfortune for the hall and its occupants, and even the recipient of the gift, as she advanced in years, found its presence increasingly intolerable. As she looked on the dusky lawn in the evenings, or when the moon was silvering the landscape, the motionless statue assumed a ghostly quality, and this suggestion impressed itself so strongly upon Mrs Taylor's imagination that its removal was deemed advisable to save her further distress.'

Other stories concerning the ghosts of Stoke Hall, tell of a young lady who attempted to elope with her lover who, being of lower class, was forbidden to marry the daughter of the hall. The girl was drowned whilst attempting to cross the stepping stones above Leadmill Bridge, where the swollen waters of the River Derwent, dragged her in and she drowned. After this tragedy the owners of the hall erected a statue in memory of their beloved daughter.

Another tale tells how a young lady was murdered by a band of Gypsies. J.Castle Hall, in a preface to his ballad entitled *The Astrologer's Daughter,* tells how he links the statue with a story he was once told by an old Gypsy who was passing through the area: 'Many and varied are the local traditions touching the origin of this statue, each more or less romantic. But probably the story of an old Gypsy near to the spot which she related to the writer excels alike in romance and antiquarian law. The old hag was in company with other Gypsies camping in the wood, and having noticed that a flower had been placed in the hand of the statue, I referred to the fact in conversation with the Gypsy, when the latter, assuming a perfect acquaintance with the matter, told her strange tale. On this strange legend of the Gypsy is founded *The Astrologer's Daughter.* And whether or not the story is altogether mythical, true it is that some 100 years ago there lived near Eyam an old man of extraordinary character, who was celebrated as an astrologer, as recorded in the works of Glover, Pendleton, and others, on the people and history of Derbyshire.'

The story concerns a young nobleman named Victor who falls in love with Flora, the daughter of a much-feared Gypsy astrologer, famous in the area for his uncanny ability to predict future events from the passage of the stars.

Flora, who was a kind and beautiful girl, met Victor in the woods one summer day and the two instantly fell in love with each other, shortly afterwards they were married. They set up home in a small cottage, above Grindleford, close to the woods where they had met. For a while the two lived a very happy life and would while away the days and nights constantly in each others company. Sadly their happiness was not to last, Victor was called away to serve his country in a war.

Twelve months passed by and Victor returned home to find the cottage was abandoned, the windows and doors standing open wide, exposing the house to all the elements. Distraught by what he had found, Victor immediately began to look about him, and there, walking through the woods, he saw his wife dressed in the purest white garments, her arms outstretched, coming towards him, J.Castle Hall, in his ballad concludes:

And then she forward leans, and Victor sees
A gush of tears fall from her eyes upon
A rose of purest whiteness that she holds
With her hand. No longer now he waits,
But quickly clasps his hand around her form.
O mystery of power and mercy, help!
His arms have through that outline passed as
through
A shadow.

Other versions of the story tell how Victor, after seeing the ghost of his wife, discovered that Flora had in fact died, nine months after he had left, giving birth to a daughter. He immediately set about trying to find the child, who had been adopted by a group of Gypsy travellers, eventually, after a further year of searching, he found her. As time went by the child grew in her mother's image, and in later years she became a great deal of comfort and consolation to Victor who, for the remainder of his life took no other bride.

In memory of his lost love Victor erected the statue of Flora, which may still be seen today standing in an ancient grove, covered in lichen and moss, her head missing from an idiotic act of vandalism. Her ghost still haunts the area, and anyone brave enough to travel near the site, especially when the moon is full, will see the statue come alive and begin to walk about.

A VISION OF DOOM

OF THE MANY curious ghost tales to be encountered within our glorious Derbyshire there is perhaps none as strange as the mysterious ghostly apparition which appeared, in a vision, to a young prince in 1501.

Arthur, elder son and heir to King Henry VII, was frequently in the habit of visiting Haddon Hall, where to this day there can still be seen an apartment named the Prince's Chamber, which displays his armorial bearings in several places. Prince Arthur was a friend of Sir Henry's son George, who later became much respected for his valiant deeds, so much respected that the locals of the shire named him the 'King of the Peak'.

When visiting Haddon Hall Prince Arthur liked nothing better than to spend his spare days wandering the local countryside, exploring the local sights and the areas immediately around the hall. One particular warm and hazy September evening in 1501, after having spent much of the day wandering along the banks of the River Wye in the direction of Bakewell, Prince Arthur reached the crossroads at Hassop where stood an ancient cross, which may now be seen outside the Vernon Chapel at All Saints churchyard, Bakewell. Being tired and fatigued by his wanderings the young Prince decided to rest for a short while at the base of the cross. There he is said to have sat, upon a green and grassy knoll, deep in thought and meditation, when suddenly before him appeared an apparition who has been described by one writer as being a 'tall thin female dressed in white; her features sunken and wan, her lips of an ashy hew, and her eyeballs protruding, bright and motionless'. The wraith stared motionless at the prince for several moments then slowly raised her hand, pointed, and in a voice that could send chills down the spine of even the most steadfast heart, uttered the following prophecy:

"Unhappy royal Prince, mourn not thy fate which is not thine! One earthly pageant awaits thee, yea, it is at hand; and then, ah! then thou wilt drop into the lap of thy mother – ah, thy mother earth! Forth comes to Britain's shore thy lovely, smiling bride – ah! bride and widow of a royal boy!"

The Bakewell Cross. Many centuries ago the ghost of a woman, with protruding eyes and ashen lips, who materialised as if from the cross, appeared in a vision to a young prince forewarning him of his own doom.

Just as the ghostly vision finished her last words, the Prince awoke. Disturbed that such a creature should enter his slumber speaking words of doom, the young Prince remained deep in thought, for the rest of his journey, wondering whether the prophecy the wraith had spoke, would indeed come to pass.

On arriving back at Haddon Hall Prince Arthur was immediately greeted by Sir Henry Vernon, who, informed him that his Spanish bride-to-be, Catherine, fourth daughter of King Ferdinand of Castile, and Aragon; whom the Prince had been betrothed to at the tender age of 12 – in the chapel of the manor of Bewdley – had arrived in England. The orders were that the prince was to return to London at once, where he was to be married without delay. The Prince instantly remembered the words of the wraith and now knowing that the first part of her prophecy had indeed come true, he feared that the remaining might also prove to be correct.

As the wedding plans were being made the Prince seemed for a while to forget his unhappy experience at the old cross until, only four months after his wedding, and not long after he had moved to his new marital home at Ludlow Castle in Shropshire, Prince Arthur fell seriously ill, an illness which he sadly did not recover from. As the wraith at the cross had foretold the young prince did indeed die, and only four months after her wedding Catherine became a widow. The last words of her husband is said to have been recorded as, "O, the vision of the cross at Haddon!"

ALSOP-EN-LE-DALE

IN ONE OF Derbyshire's most beautiful areas lies the quaint village of Alsop-en-le-Dale. Not too far from this village is a house known as Hanson Grange. In the area that immediately surrounds this house there can be heard the pitiful sounds of a man crying and pleading for his life to be spared. On other occasions people have reported hearing what sounds like several men violently fighting, although at no time has anyone physically seen anyone. So convinced were one couple that they searched the whole area, several times over, before they were convinced that there was no one playing a trick on them.

Hanson Grange is known to have a history of hauntings which date back to 1467 when, John Mycock was murdered there. His death was caused by four men, John de la Pole of Hartington, who struck him on the side of the head, Henry Vigurs of Monyash, who stabbed him in the breast, Mathew Bland of Hartington, who struck him with a staff and John Harrison who shot an arrow in his back.

There are no records to ascertain why this foul incident took place, but we do know that the four men were summoned to appear before the King in 1649, but all of the four murderers failed to appear before the court. Today should you be travelling near Hanson Grange, especially I am informed in the autumn, then do not be surprised if you too hear the ghostly sounds of a bloody murder taking place.

FLORENCE NIGHTINGALE

FLORENCE NIGHTINGALE was the second child of Edward William Shaw, who later changed his name to Nightingale. He named Florence after the famous Italian city in which she was born. Her father inherited a great deal of property amongst which was Lea Hurst, a 17th-century gabled farmhouse which has been altered a great deal over the years. Later he built Willersley Castle, overlooking the River Derwent, which he later sold to Sir Richard Arkwright for £20,000.

Within her lifetime Florence Nightingale became a legend. Her international recognition came during the Crimean War. So disturbed was Florence by the horrors of war that she could barely tear herself away from the sick and the dying who nicknamed her 'The Lady with the Lamp'. In April 1856 Florence returned home to Derbyshire.

Many of the local people were poised to celebrate her return, to pay homage to a woman who had done so much for so little. Arriving back in Derbyshire Florence quietly slipped through the myriad of watching eyes and made her way back to Lea Hurst. For the next 50 years

Lea Hurst. The ghost of Florence Nightingale is seen to wander the house and gardens.

Florence Nightingale. Known in life and death as 'The Lady with the Lamp'.

Florence was to change the face of nursing, consistently petitioning government for medical changes within the country. Florence died on 13 August 1910.

Lea Hurst remained the home of the Nightingale family until Louis Nightingale died in 1940, the house was later sold at auction. In 1951 Lea Hurst was presented to the Royal Surgical Aid Society, who then used the building as a home for the elderly.

Lea Hurst is believed to be haunted by several spirits, perhaps the most prolific is that of Florence Nightingale who is known to have loved the house a great deal. Her ghost is said to be seen wandering along a top corridor and down the stairs. The gardens are also haunted by Florence who appears to be inspecting the plants and flowers in the borders and beds. Her ghost is also said to haunt several other buildings in Derbyshire. The Derbyshire Royal Infirmary is where the ghost of Florence has been seen wandering along the corridors. At one time her appearances were so frequent that staff working at the hospital nicknamed the phantom 'The Lady with the Lamp' as she appeared to be always carrying a light. Other members of staff reported seeing the ghost looking at patients on several of the older wards. When staff approached the phantom, believing that it was a doctor or another nurse, the lady simply vanished before their eyes.

Vengeful Spirits

BEELEY MOOR —
HOB HURST'S HOUSE

THREE miles south-east of Baslow, on the edge of East Moor, can be found a Bronze Age round barrow, surrounded by a ditch and a bank, which is thought to date from 1600 to 1000BC.

Being one of the least known prehistoric sites in Derbyshire and the Peak District, perhaps due to its relative inaccessibility, the round barrow stands 1,000ft above sea-level and is best approached by motor car via Beeley Village then Upper Load, then taking the footpath, which leads directly to the site.

This rather spectacular Bronze Age burial mound is 32ft in diameter and is surrounded by a ditch measuring 9ft in width and an unusually high bank of earth measuring 4ft originally thought to have been higher. The whole site encloses an area of approximately 70ft. The barrow when excavated was found to consist mainly of sand and gritstone. L.V.Grinsell in *Ancient Mounds of England* (1936) records how:

'The height of the bank relative to that of, the barrow, even before it was excavated, is very much greater than one would normally expect and it would appear that either the people who built the monument surrounded it with an unusually high bank or, for some reason, denudation of the bank has not taken place at the same rate as that of the mound. It is almost certain that the former is the fact and that the barrow when first constructed did not stand much above the surrounding bank of earth.'

A 3ft deep indentation, located at the top of the central mound, remains as a scar of excavation when the site was opened by local archaeologist Thomas Bateman, in June 1853. Bateman cut a trench from the south side into the mound where he discovered a stone-lined grave, composed of gritstone, measuring 10ft 3ins by 9ft. Inside Bateman discovered the remains of an inhumation, together with two pieces of burnt lead ore, 'lying in the very spot where they had been drawn together while the embers of the funeral pyre were glowing'. Surrounding the scorched human bones were small sandstone boulders, arranged in a semicircular position. The practise of marking off the dead with such stones is rare in this part of England, generally being more common in the south. The name given to the burial mound indicates the ancient belief that such places were once believed to be the homes of fairies and goblins. When the results of the archaeological excavation was published by Bateman, telling of the bones that were found within the site, it refuelled the belief in Hob Hurst and devils that ate children.

Hob Hurst however was well known to our ancestors, especially farmers, who, according to folklore, would leave quantities of food and milk in the fire hearth in a bid to placate this spirit of nature. Hob was known to wreak havoc with those who upset him, cutting down a sacred tree or constructing a wall over Hob's land was sure to infuriate him. When Hob was bad, he was extremely unpleasant and would cause havoc for anyone he took a disliking to. However when Hob was good he was magical, often he would take to working at night time, doing favourable things to please his espoused acquaintance. R.M. Litchfield in his *Tales of the Peak* demonstrates how a lonely old woman helped the spirit Hob when he needed a home: 'And so the sprite took up his abode with the old woman, and never was the house cleaner nor the old woman happier, for all the day long she talked to him as she went about her spinning and her other tasks, and he would answer with a sigh as of the wind through

Hob Hurst's House on Beeley Moor. A place which has for centuries had a reputation for being the haunt of demonic forces.

long grass, or chuckle like a moorland stream in its bed. She was careful not to look directly at him, for hobs are very shy creatures and soon take fright, but if she watched carefully from the corner of her eye she would often see a small, brown, bony figure perched in the corner, head on knees, staring into the fire, or watching her with glittering little eyes. At night while she slept he would clean the house right through, and bake oatcakes, which the old woman loved to eat, fresh and warm when she rose.

As summer came in the hob would follow her outside while she worked in her garden, and took up his seat far inside the rocks where a small spring flowed out of the hillside. Who knows that there wasn't a natural spirit living deep in the rock, a spirit of the water the hob met with, for the old woman found that the water flowed faster

and clearer and tasted sweeter after Hob came to live with her. She drank more of it, and bathed in it often, and soon found that her step became lighter and her aches and pains seemed to be less. Some days she felt herself to be a girl again.

Other place names, in Derbyshire and the Peak District, still reflect the once widely held belief in the supernatural creature. Hob Hurst's House in Monsal Dale is a huge rocky outcrop and a cave where it was once believed a giant lived. Locals, in times past, would not venture near the site for fear of meeting something not of this world.

In Deep Dale, near King Sterndale, Hob's House has become Thirst House Cave. The waters of a nearby spring, having been blessed by the spirit of Hob, are reputed to have miraculous healing powers if taken before sunset on Good Friday.

THE WINNATS PASS, CASTLETON

THIS dramatic limestone gorge was once a major entrance to Castleton, carrying the salt route from Cheshire to Yorkshire. The Winnats Pass, once written 'Wyndeyates' meaning the pass through which the wind

sweeps, has for centuries had a reputation for being haunted by several ghosts, perhaps the two most frequently seen ghosts are that of a young couple who were murdered there several centuries ago.

In the middle of the 18th century, Peak Forest

was the Gretna Green of England. The vicar, who was not under the jurisdiction of a Bishop, could marry couples at any time of the day or night, and eloping hopefuls would come from far and wide for the pleasure.

One such couple were Alan and Clara who were deeply in love. But alas, Clara's parents would have none of it, her father went to great extremes to keep them apart, even to the extent of threatening to shoot Alan if he went within as much as a mile of his daughter, principally because Alan was a penniless labourer.

Their love was so deep for each other that one calm moonlit night, in 1748, they set off from their native Scotland to take the long perilous journey to the Peak Forest, in Derbyshire.

Through the elements they travelled. Day in, day out, until eventually the weary travellers arrived at Castleton, where they decided to stay the night at an inn, and to ask further directions from the innkeeper. Seated in the inn were five burly miners who fell silent when the young couple asked the innkeeper which way they

should go. It appears to be at this point that the five miners, who had guessed Clara's wealth from the expensive clothes she wore, hatched a plan to relieve the young couple of their possessions.

After retiring to bed at the inn Clara had a terrible dream. In it, she and Alan were riding through a rocky gorge, where they were attacked by robbers. As she watched she saw their assailants murder Alan, they then turned their attention on her. At this point she woke up in a cold sweat. She immediately awoke Alan and told him about her dream, he lovingly reassured her that it was nothing to worry about.

Early the next morning, the five miners were at the Winnats Pass, awaiting the arrival of the couple.

Arriving at the Winnats Pass, Clara became uneasy, an icy chill went down her spine as she recognised the gorge, from her dream, it was all that she could do to continue. Alan, noticing her discomfort, reassured her that everything would be fine, and they continued picking their way, on horseback, through the stony pathway, every step

The Winnatts Pass, Castleton. The ghostly screams of two murdered lovers can still be heard echoing down the pass on windy nights.

a step closer to their doom. Halfway through the Winnats, the five marauders leapt from their hiding places and, seizing the young lovers, dragged them from their horses to a nearby shack where they demanded money. Alan put up a fight and in the process was brutally axed to death. Realising their crime the now murderers went outside to discuss what should be done with Clara. Knowing that they could not let her go, they re-entered the shack where they took it in turns to rape and abuse her, regardless of her pitiful cries for them to stop, they then murdered the unfortunate Clara in cold blood.

Silent now, the full realisation of their crimes upon them, the five miners left the battered lifeless bodies of the two young lovers on the shack floor, and parted their ways deciding to come back later that night to share the money the young couple had been carrying (£200), then dispose of their bodies. At midnight the five returned and, approaching the shack, they heard sounds coming from within. Frightened out of their wits, the miners fled. The forthcoming night, the same thing happened again, and again on the third night. On the fourth night, full of false courage from the amount of alcohol they had consumed earlier, the miners managed to enter the shack, and wrapping the two bodies in old sackcloth, buried them in the dead of night where, they thought, no man would ever find them.

Distributing the money which they had killed for, the five parted ways, glad to see the back of the Winnats Pass.

Four days later, Alan and Clara's horses were found wandering near the pass. There was little doubt in many of the locals minds that some dreadful misfortune had befallen the young couple. A diligent investigation managed to turn up nothing, and the murderers' identities remained unknown. Very soon after this terrible event, strange noises were said to be heard coming from somewhere central in the Winnats Pass. Locals told of blood curdling screams, strange thudding noises and the distinct sound of something being dragged. Stories were also being told of the ghosts of a young couple, seen clambering up the rocky sides of the Winnats, or of two young people hand in hand, who would suddenly appear and then incomprehensively disappear. Tongues began to wag, and although the local community as good as knew that the young couple had been murdered and who their murderers were, no one was ever brought before the courts. A decade after this terrible event, two skeletons were found wedged in a mine shaft in the Winnats Pass, it was widely believed that these were the remains of the two young lovers.

The fate of the five miners was already cast; some unspoken curse lay upon them, and one by one they eventually all paid the price for their crime. The first, Nicholas Cook, died within a year. The second, John Bradshaw, was one day walking through the Winnats Pass when something so frightened him that he clambered up the side of a gorge where the wind took him and dashed his body on the rocks. The third, Thomas Hall, took his own life. The fourth, Francis Butley, was also in the Winnats when something not of this world confronted him. Scrambling to get away, a boulder, which seemed to fall from the skies, crushed the life from his body. Finally the fifth man, James Ashton, persecuted by his crime and almost insane made a death bed confession to the vicar of Castleton. Although the fifth man's death came late, it was probably the worst of the five, for he died lonely, guilty and afraid of what he might meet on the other side.

Today there are still reports of ghosts being seen in the pass. On moonlit nights, the ghosts of the two young lovers can still be seen trying to escape from the Winnats Pass, by scrambling up the sides of a cliff. There are also occasional reports of terrible screams being heard. Clara's saddle may still be seen in the gift shop at the Speedwell Cavern.

THE CASTLE HOTEL, CASTLETON

THE CASTLE HOTEL at Castleton has long had an association with ghosts. According to the owner of the public house it is haunted by numerous ghosts which frequently put in an appearance. The most prolific ghost is said to be that of a jilted bride who has been seen walking along one of the corridors within the building.

Another spectral visitor is an old lady who appears bathed in grey, always in the upper parts of the building and always in the evening. A third ghost that haunts the building is a gentleman in a pinstriped suit. He has been seen on dozens of occasions, normally standing near to a large fireplace in a front room of the pub.

I had chance to visit the property on a ghost hunt. Having arrived at the building I was instantly struck by its friendliness and charm. The landlord and landlady reiterated several stories of odd experiences they had been forced to suffer. Several members of staff had been pushed whilst serving in one of the back bars. Another female member of staff once felt her bottom being pinched by an obviously amorous ghost, when she turned around to see who her assailant was she discovered only herself to be present in the bar. Although I could not personally sense any ghosts within the building I was assured by the owners that the spirits, and I do not mean the alcoholic type, were very real.

ANCHOR CHURCH, INGLEBY

ANCHOR Church is an ancient sandstone cave which over the centuries has been enlarged to include two rooms with windows. Standing on a section of the River Trent between Ingleby and Foremark, known as Black Pool, Anchor Church has a long history of being haunted by several spirits, the legend associated with the ghosts that haunt the vicinity is a particularly tragic one.

According to an ancient document entitled *The Severed Hand of Johanne with the Long Hair: a Legend of Knowle Hills and Anchor Church,* there once existed a grand castle at Knowle Hills, near Ticknall, about the middle of the 12th century. The castle belonged to Sir Hugo and Lady Johanne de Burdett who, having been matched in marriage by their parents, are said to have existed in total bliss. So happy were the couple together that even the wife of King Henry II, Eleanor, is quoted as having frequently said to her husband "There are few couples in your domain that set so good an example as Sir Hugo and his Johanne".

The couple lived happily for a time until an evil man known as Baron Boyvill of Castleton, cousin to Sir Hugo met and secretly lusted after the beautiful Lady Johanne. So intent was the Baron on dividing the two, that he set about persuading Sir Hugo to abandon his home, become a crusader, and join the growing numbers of knights who were responding to the call of the Holy War. Suspecting what the evil Baron was plotting, Lady Johanne pleaded with her husband to stay in England, informing him that she was displeased with the effect Baron Boyvill was having on him.

For a short while Johanne's pleas appeared to work, Sir Hugo temporarily forgot about the Holy War and Johanne was content to go back to the way they had been living before the arrival of Baron Boyvill. However, not content to leave the loving couple alone, Baron Boyvill enlisted the help of a monk named Father Bernard, who the evil Baron encouraged to pay regular visits to a Monastery of Black Canons at Repton.

Sir Hugo was often in the habit of visiting Repton, frequently venturing near the monastery gates where monks arriving home from the Holy War would reiterate their tales of battles and bloodshed. Sir Hugo would listen eagerly to the stories and, became increasingly downhearted at not being able to go to the crusades, so downhearted that eventually he decided to seek spiritual guidance of a monk, Father Bernard, who had by this time made himself well acquainted with Sir Hugo.

Shortly after making the decision to seek guidance on the matter, Sir Hugo met with the friar who, having already been primed with his reply by Baron Boyvill, strongly advised him that it was his duty to go to war, furthermore it was almost certainly what God desired. Before leaving Father Bernard handed over a sachet of sleeping draught to Sir Hugo, advising him to administer the drug to his wife the night before he left, lest she should weaken his resolve to go. Several weeks later Johanne awoke one morning from a troubled sleep to discover that her beloved husband had gone and hanging around her neck was a gold locket with the words 'five years' inscribed upon it, her husband had left to join the crusades!

On discovering that her husband had departed for the wars, Lady Johanne immediately became distraught, for three long years she is said to have existed in a state of depression and unhappiness and to pass the lonely hours away, she took to embroidering an altar cloth. The threads for the embroidering were made from her own beautiful long hair which she mixed with strands of gold and silver, the pattern intricately depicting insects, birds, trees, fruits and flowers. When the altar cloth was finished Lady Johanne planned to place it on the altar of Our Lady of Repton, as a thanks offering for her husband's safe return. However, all hopes for Sir Hugo's safe return were shattered when news reached her, via Father Bernard, that he had been taken prisoner by the Turks, who were holding him to ransom.

Taking only a short while to gather all the gold necessary to secure her husband's release, Lady Johanne immediately dispatched the fortune with the monk. As the days passed into weeks and they in turn into months, she became increasingly anxious taking to sitting by the window of her room watching for any sign of his return. A year passed by when, one morning, glancing from her window Lady Johanne saw an armed figure, upon horseback, riding up the avenue and into the courtyard. Upon the rider's breast was the symbol of a red cross, sign of the crusades. Believing the mysterious figure to be that of her husband, she ran with open arms to greet him and to her horror discovered that it was Baron de Boyvill. Without, hesitation the evil Baron immediately began to tell Lady Johanne that all that had been handed over for the gold and silver, was the dead body of her beloved Sir Hugo. Little sympathy was shown for the heartbroken widow, instead the Baron informed her that, considering the fact Sir Hugo had no heir, he was now the rightful owner of the castle and all the lands that went with it. Furthermore he would allow her stay on at the castle if she agreed to be his wife. Struck by horror at his suggestions, Lady Johanne promptly and flatly refused, stating that she would take no other, as a result of this statement the Baron imprisoned her within the castle for a period of five years.

When the period of her confinement had elapsed Johanne was informed that she was to become the Baron's bride. The Baron immediately left the castle to invite and collect guests to the marriage, a marriage that she knew she could not hold off any longer. Suddenly the door to her room was flung open and there, silhouetted in the doorway was the love she had thought she would never see again, Sir Hugo. As he entered the room Johanne knew from his countenance and the expression upon his face that something was wrong, "Unfaithful woman" he cried accusingly "betrayer of thy husband, thy hour of punishment is at hand." As soon as these words had been spoken, Sir Hugo drew his sword and clasping the unfortunate Johanne by the arm he stuck a blow which severed her hand, adding the words "This hand on which I placed a bridal ring shall be the sacrifice of thy infidelity, thus I immolate my revenge." Turning away from where Lady Johanne lay bleeding to death, Sir Hugo marched from the room. Later that day Sir Hugo met with Baron de Boyvill, in the woods, where he was returning from his task of inviting guests to the wedding. A terrible battle is said to have taken place, the result being that Sir Hugo killed Baron de Boyvill and left him where he fell, later his corpse was eaten by wolves, which were known to have been numerous in the region at that time.

Many years passed by in which time Sir Hugo led the life of a recluse, never marrying and rarely venturing out of his castle. One stormy night a messenger arrived at the castle asking to speak to the owner. Reluctantly Sir Hugo granted him council. The messenger implored Sir Hugo to go with him to a cave nearby, known as Anchor Church, where an elderly monk, whose death was imminent, was asking to see Sir Hugo.

It was widely known that the monk at Anchor Church was a pious man who had chosen a segregated life of poverty and prayer. It was also rumoured that terrible screams of anguish, pain and cries of forgiveness could often be heard coming from the cave. So pious was the monk that he had received a reputation for being a miracle worker and pilgrims suffering from many maladies sought him out. Sir Hugo agreed to go with the messenger and arriving at the cave found the monk at the point of death. The monk immediately recognised Sir Hugo and grasping at his hand begged him for his forgiveness, adding

that it was he who had brought about the downfall of Lady Johanne. Once Sir Hugo had assured the monk of his forgiveness, the frail and tortured figure reached beneath his robes and produced a parchment, no sooner had he handed the piece of paper over, then he took his last breath. Unable to translate the contents of the letter Sir Hugo hastened to Repton Monastery where a monk read to him the following:

'The mendicant monk friar Bernard and the recluse of the Trent are one and the same. Worldly vanity seduced me to crime – I wished to be thought a saint and I have been a wretched sinner. I travelled over Europe to gain partisans to the cause. I gathered money and spent it in wickedness instead of charity. The Baron of Boyvill paid me to gain over Sir Hugo de Burdett and I accompany'd both to the Holy Land. I betrayed Sir Hugo to the paynim's hands and after obtaining money for his ransom from his lady, I returned with the sum which I shared with the Baron and found means to let Sir Hugo know that his lady was false and refused to ransom him. After this the Baron came back to England and endeavoured by representing that her husband was dead to induce the Lady Johanne to become his wife, which she steadfastly refused. I had obtained large sums from the Baron, but of late had refused to give me more and in the end I wrought his ruin. I procured the release of Sir Hugo by my agents and sent him word that his wife and friend were both false. He encountered the Baron in the woods of Foremark and slew him, for he taunted him with having gained the affections of his wife. Mad with jealousy, Sir Hugo put the innocent lady to death. Remorse almost drove me distracted when I found the effect of my work, and I strove by penitence to atone for my dreadful sins and those I had caused. Pray for my soul, and let masses be said for one otherwise lost for ever.'

On hearing the words of the written confession Sir Hugo's heart filled with intense

Anchor Church. Haunt of a phantom monk who is condemned to wander the earth for his evil deeds.

grief and, returning to his castle, proceeded immediately to Johanne's room, which he had not entered since her death. There he discovered the inscribed gold locket, which he had placed about her neck before he had left for the crusades, lying upon the embroidered alter cloth. He stayed in the room all night, clutching the heart and the cloth, bewailing his outcast state and asking God for forgiveness.

At sunrise Sir Hugo wandered into the courtyard, where Lady Johanne's body had, been interred and, kneeling by her grave, he made a solemn vow of everlasting love, adding that as long as life was held within his body he would take no other as his wife. No sooner were his words spoken then a nightingale, perched in a tree nearby, burst into beautiful song. Taking this to be a sign from God, Sir Hugo, according to legend, followed the bird until eventually he reached Ancote in Warwickshire and there built a monastery in expiation of his crime. Upon the altar of the new monastery was draped the

exquisite embroidered cloth that the Lady Johanne had made from her own hair and, thereafter, people with maladies of the hands would make a pilgrimage to the holy shrine where many are said to have been cured of their afflictions.

Two ancient stone carved heads once existed at a farm near Repton until the previous owner moved to another part of Derbyshire and is thought to have taken the heads with them. There were originally three heads which were believed to represent the three main characters in the legend of the Lady Johanne for the ancient script concludes: 'and all that remains of the old building is now formed into a pleasure house – where usually not a sound is heard but the wind amongst the old trees, and the rustle of the ivy waving to and fro along the old wall, where you see that strange face carved, that seems as if it were looking over the battlements watching what is going on. Some say on moonlit nights the whole figure has been seen, and it looks like a knight in armour as it walks in stately step, all around this green, where once stood a tower, and it pauses at a little doorway, utters a deep sigh and vanishes. There were two old women who once lived here and they used to hear and see strange things, chains rattling, and, screams and groans that were awful. One of the old women died and used to come back to the other and tell wonderful secrets, so she said. But she went, too, and nothing out of the common ever happens now.'

Today many people still believe Anchor Church, and Knowle Hills, to be haunted by the four main characters of this ancient legend. On moonlit nights it is said that a ghostly white hand can be seen gliding about by itself. One gentleman, who frequently camped at the site, of Anchor Church as a youth, recalls how he 'was awakened one night by the sounds of a man crying. Believing that his friend, who had accompanied him, was having a bad dream, he threw an empty bottle at him to wake him up. The friend without moving from his sleeping bag answered "It is not me!", both froze with horror

as they realised that the noise was actually coming from just outside the cave. Neither dared go outside to investigate and for many minutes they sat there listening to the pitiful crying until eventually it simply faded away. Even after the sounds of crying had gone the two sat there terrified that it might come back and when the morning light finally broke the darkness of the night they made haste to get away from the cave as quickly as possible. Other sightings of ghosts have taken place in the vicinity. Fishermen have reported seeing the ghostly figure of a woman in white seen gliding along the river bank. Ghostly sounds of people fighting and crying have also been heard.

Of recent years there has been talk of 'Black Masses' being acted out at the site. Other, so-called, witches are also believed to have worshipped at the cave. This unfortunately is a shame as Anchor Church is a very beautiful tourist spot and it would be very sad if this little-known and wonderful cave became a beacon for less desirable individuals.

HIGHLOW HALL

ONCE said by local historian Roy Christian to be 'Reputedly the most haunted house in Derbyshire', the ghosts of Highlow Hall now seem almost gone. Not that much unusual happens at the hall these days, but at one time there were reports of many phantoms, so much so that television cameras were installed at the hall to try and capture the spectres on film – needless to say this failed.

The main ghost that once haunted the hall dates back to the 14th century, when it is said that the scheming Nicholas Eyre, who earlier in his life had murdered a stone mason, wooed two sisters of the last male heir of the Archer family,

in a devious plan to claim their inheritance. Falling in love with the elder of the sisters Nicholas planned to marry her, and when the younger sister discovered his betrayal she fled the hall never to be seen again. Seen again alive, that is. Several months after the Archer sister had fled the house, Nicholas married her elder sister. All went well for a few years until one day the younger sister's ghost appeared at the hall. Nicholas is said to have watched the ghastly phantom walk down the stairs, where turning to face him she shrieked:

"You think to rear up sons around you, and each of these sons to increase his lands by marriage to the best families in Derbyshire, until the heirs shall be lords of the shire. True, these sons should be born and there sons to the 15th generation. Some of their brows shall be adorned with coronets, their acres shalt be by the thousands, they shall connect themselves with the best

Highlow Hall. Once reputed to be the most haunted house in Derbyshire.

blood of the county – but my curse shall be upon them! There shall come events which will crush determination itself, however honourable, and leave them without rood or soil."

Everything the ghost predicted happened. Over the following generations the Eyres became lords of more than 20 manors, and were related by marriage to some of the most influential people of Derbyshire. By 1842 their fortunes had gone and the curse of the jilted ghost had indeed come to pass.

Another ghost that was reputed to haunt the hall was that of a 'white lady', who was seen on several occasions wandering the outer grounds of the hall. No one knows who this ghost might be, local legend has it that she is a previous owner of the hall who was murdered in an upstairs bedroom, her body then being dragged, across the landing and down the stairs, for many years after people reported hearing the ghostly re-enactment.

In 1911, a carter from Dronfield, who had been delivering a load to the village of Abney, and was returning home past the hall at two o'clock in the morning, reported seeing the ghost of a lady in white with her hands resting on the cattle trough, staring into the water. A farmer living nearby would often tell the tale of how he would frequently see the ghost crossing the old courtyard of the house, apparently oblivious to his presence, even when he touched his cap and uttered the greeting "Goodnight, missus".

Since 1978, Highlow Hall has been filmed, photographed, staked out, and had numerous so called psychics attempt to encourage the ghosts to appear. All this has been to no avail, the ghosts are staying quiet. When I visited the hall several years ago I was informed by the occupants that the ghosts were more than welcome to stay, even if they have stopped bothering to show themselves.

The haunted staircase at Highlow Hall. The ghost of a 'White Lady', believed to be a jilted lover, appears to walk down the stairs on certain nights of the year.

KINDER SCOUT

FOR GENERATIONS Kinder Scout has, according to many a legend, been reputed to be haunted by a myriad of ghosts. Mermaids, water spirits, boggarts, werewolves, white ladies and phantom dogs, to name but a few. Kinder Scout, a popular summer walking spot, is a wild and barren place where the wind can reach such a force in autumn and winter, as to make walking almost impossible. There are some terrific walks with many breathtaking views of the surrounding moorland and countryside. The chief elevations of Kinder Scout are: Kinder Low 2,088ft; Crowden Head 2,070, and Fairbrook Naze 2,049.

Perhaps the most famous ghost story concerning the area is that of the ghost, or water nymph, that has been seen at the base of Kinder Downfall in an expanse of water, shown on ordnance maps, known as 'The Mermaid's Pool'. The Kinder Downfall, at the foot of the famous Rock Down-

fall, is one of a few waterfalls in the area, taking place when there has been copious amounts of rainfall and, according to one legend, the appearance of the mermaid is often synchronised with the downfall. The poet Henry Kirke described the mermaid as having great beauty:

Kinder Scout. According to local legend the area around Kinder Scout is the haunt of a Roman soldier, a boggart, a werewolf and a mermaid.

'Her golden hair fell o'er her shoulders white,
And curled in amorous ringlets round her
   breasts
Her eyes were melting into love, her lips
Made the very roses envious;
Withal a voice so full, and yet so clear,
So tender, made for loving dialogues'.

The pool itself is an acidic mire, said to hold no life within its waters where no living creature will drink from its edges. Those wishing to see the mermaid should visit the pool on Easter Eve, when midnight strikes into Easter Sunday when she is said to rise from the waters and transmit to those who would dare seek her out, the gift of eternal life. Those she finds no favour in are dragged beneath the waters to their deaths. One gentleman, a soldier named Aaron Ashton, of Hayfield, was at one time a regular visitor to the pool and is recorded as having lived to the ripe old age of 104, alas he died in 1835 and there are no records stating whether he ever saw the mermaid or not.

Water spirits were widely believed in by the Celts who were known to have regularly made sacrifices to water gods in the belief that this action would placate them, thus ensuring a purer water supply. Another supernatural belief concerning the Mermaid's Pool is that if you stare into the murky depths of the pool for long enough the future will be revealed in a series of visions appearing on the water.

The whole area surrounding Kinder Scout is steeped in ghost stories and legends including Roman soldiers who haunt the lonely moorland expanse known as Bleaklow, a werewolf said to be heard howling whenever there is a full moon and a phantom bomber plane seen silently flying across the area. The ghostly Roman Soldiers do not show themselves to people, but instead are said to be heard marching across the lonely moorlands on dark, cold winter nights. Local farmers also tell the tale of the 'Kinder Boggart' seen roaming the area around Kinder Downfall, striking terror into the hearts of those that see him. Then there is 'Peggy with th'lantern', as she is known locally, who is seen high on the moors, appearing as a yellow light, enticing foolish followers to their deaths high on the summit of Lantern Pike.

ASHFORD-IN-THE-WATER THE GHOSTS OF HULAC WARREN AND HEDESSA

HEDESSA was a beautiful young shepherdess and was said to have been one of the fairest daughters of mortal man, and being kind, considerate, and loving towards the beasts of the fields, the gods favoured her and would often guide a lost animal back to her rather than have her seek to find the creature in dark woods or coppice. Hedessa was engaged to a young man whom she loved with all her heart and was more than happy with her simple life of tending her animals, and planning for the day that she would marry the man she loved.

For some time Hedessa had been pursued by a man called Hulac Warren, who was said to have been a giant of a man and who was also accustomed to having his own way. Hulac had planned to take Hedessa whether she liked it or not, for he was tormented by lust and want for the young beauty, secretly following her wherever she went.

One warm evening Hedessa was walking home through a valley called Demon's Dale, by the River Wye, in the parish of Taddington. Hulac Warren, who had concealed himself in some woody undergrowth, sprang out from where he was hiding and snatched the young Hedessa, who he intended to have his wicked way with. Hedessa, realising what Hulac's intentions were began to weep, and called out to the gods pleading that they might spare her from his evil designs.

Having the ear of the gods, her face finding favour in their eyes, they heard and answered her plea, allowing her to be momentarily released from Hulac's grasp, Hedessa, realising her chance, ran from him and threw herself from a precipice to a stony death at the foot of the cliff. Immediately, near to the place where she fell, a spring of pure water, as pure as her soul, some say, gushed forth.

Hulac was furious that he had been denied his chance to have the woman that he had longed for, so furious that he began to curse the gods, shouting abuse and swearing his hatred for them.

The gods, hearing his words of anger, looked down in distaste at Hulac and for his monstrous crime against Hedessa they turned him into a stone, there he has remained to this day lying in a bend of the River Wye, near Ashford-in-the-Water, as a reminder to all those who would provoke the anger of the gods.

The legend of Hedessa and Hulac Warren is certainly of ancient origin and seems likely to be of pagan descent. Even to this day locals still believe the site to be haunted by all manner of ghouls and spirits, several centuries ago people would not go near the Warren Stone, as it is now known, for fear of meeting something not of this world. There is still the old superstition of spitting when passing this point, the belief being that to do so inhibits any evil force, that may come from the rock, attaching itself to the traveller.

Myths
and
Magic

PEVERIL CASTLE

KNOWN as the Castle of the Peak, Peveril Castle is situated high above the beautiful and historic village of Castleton. According to the Domesday Book in 1086, it was recorded for the first time as the Castle of the Peak. Apart from being the only preserved remains of a Norman castle in Derbyshire, it is also recorded as one of the best preserved in England. The castle was once immortalised by Sir Walter Scott in his novel *Peveril of the Peak*. The land was originally held by the Saxons and in 1086, along with a great deal of other property passed to William Peveril the illegitimate son of William the Conqueror. Shortly after he came into possession of the castle he set about reinforcing it with stone, one of the first castles to be built in this way. The northern wall which faces Castleton is one of the remaining walls from this time, whilst the zigzag pathway seen at the castle today, replaced a much older entrance which consisted of a wooden bridge located above the entrance to Peak Cavern near the west wall.

According to one legend the castle was once the scene of a tournament held by William Peveril in order to secure a husband for his daughter Millie. She did not wish to marry just any knight, insisting that she would only marry the one who could prove his strength by defeating all of the other competitors. The final winner was a knight named Guarine de Metz, who also managed to secure for himself the Salop Castle after he had defeated the Baron of Burgoyne.

The castle was on several occasions used as a prison. In 1402, towards the end of the castle's use, it was used as a prison for Godfrey Rowland, a Derby-

Peveril Castle. A white knight and a disembodied hand haunt this site.

shire Squire. Having petitioned parliament against an injustice and failed, he was set upon by several people who ransacked his home, at Mickel-Longsdon, then later took him to Peveril Castle. When Godfrey and his assailants arrived at the castle they 'kept him six days without meal or drink and then, cutting off his right hand, sent him adrift.'

Most of the ghosts experienced at Peveril Castle are said to be felt rather than seen. The whole castle is alleged to sometimes take on a strange chilling atmosphere and, when walking about the site, it is not hard to imagine the area to be haunted.

The main ghost that haunts the building is that of a white knight who has been seen standing near the ramparts. A second ghost is said to be that of an old lady, stories also abound of a phantom dog and also a horse which have been seen and heard in an area close to the keep, which was added to the castle in 1176. Strange noises are often said to emanate from the ruined castle, as too are the sounds of a lady singing. One lady visitor to the site claims to have seen a disembodied hand floating about in the air, perhaps the ghostly hand is that of Godfrey Rowland.

THE EAGLE STONE

THE NAME EAGLE is thought to be a corruption of Aigle, a giant Celtic god who, was known to throw huge boulders around the countryside. The Eagle Stone, which is much eroded by the elements, is to be found at Baslow Edge, near Wellington's Monument, across the moor from which can be found the Nelson Monument. The name may also be derived from the word Egglestone which interprets as Witch Stone. On certain days of the year the Eagle Stone is said to turn around at cock crow. The same legend is also associated with two other rocks in the Derbyshire area, the first is the Turning Stone near Ashover, whilst the second is known by several names, its two most popular being Stump John, or the Head Stone, which can be located on the Hallam Moors near Sheffield.

There was once a tradition amongst men from the nearby village of Baslow of climbing the stone, This was done amongst much ceremony as the girls of the village would not accept the advances of any man unless he demonstrated his

The Eagle Stone. Legend has it that this haunted stone turns around at cock-crow.

manhood by scaling the awkwardly shaped boulder. Any man managing to climb to the summit of the rock was believed to receive the blessing of the spirits — some versions of the legend say witches, which were thought to inhabit the stone.

THE WISHING STONE

The Lumsdale Wishing Stone. A nature spirit is to dwell within the stone.

HIGH above Lumsdale, near Matlock, can be found a large solitary rock which for hundreds of years has been locally referred to as the 'Wishing Stone'.

The stone, which was once very popular with the Victorians who travelled in their droves to see the huge rock, is now partly vandalised and much overshadowed by the encroaching weeds and undergrowth.

Many people journeyed to the stone in the hope of having a wish granted, for it was believed that a nature spirit dwelt in the rock. To entice the spirit to favour your request, it was necessary to perform the small ritual of walking around the rock three times, each time repeating under your breath the desired wish. It was further held that you could wish for anything you like as long as it was not money or material gain. If the nature spirit favoured your request your wish was sure to come true within the next three lunar cycles.

THE BRADWELL GHOST

IN THE 18th century there existed near Bradwell a house which was known as Hills Head, where in 1760, the body of a murdered girl was discovered under the staircase. Not long after the gruesome discovery was made her ghost began to manifest itself in the house and surrounding countryside. Dozens of people claimed to have seen the wraith, which eventually became so troublesome that the villagers refused to go out after darkness fell, for fear of meeting the ghost. Eventually, pushed to the extremes, the villagers decided to enlist the help of a local man who was known to be well versed in the practice of sorcery.

When the would-be exorcist arrived at the haunted house he was greeted by a large crowd of villagers who had gathered to witness the ritual. As soon as he walked into the house he knelt down on the floor, and, producing a piece of white chalk from his pocket, drew a large circle on the floor. Next he began to chant in prayer, at this point sweat was seen to clearly run down his face. Many of the onlookers declared afterwards that they 'felt the floor move up and down in quick succession', at which point the exorcist shouted loudly "Beroald, Beroald, Balbin, Gab, Gabor Agaba." This ancient spell is said to mean 'Arise! Arise! I charge and command, thee!' No sooner had these words been spoken than the ghost of the young girl appeared, at which point the exorcist demanded and commanded that the spirit leave the house immediately. Furthermore that she take up a new residence at The Lumb, a part of the village where a stream, Bradwell Brook, appears. There she was to remain in the form of a fish. Once a year the ghost was to be allowed to take the form of an Ousel and, for exercise, she would be allowed to fly to Lumbly Pool, a few miles away. From that time onwards the villagers were no longer troubled by the ghost.

Another story concerning Bradwell, this time dating from the 1780s, is connected with a mining disaster and tells how two brothers, Sam and William, were walking home together, late one moonlit night, when they came upon a huge black phantom dog. Suddenly Sam froze and called out to his brother to stop and, pointing in the direction of the huge creature, he asked his brother if he could see it, but William could not.

Sam watched in horror as the creature began to move towards him. It came so close that he could feel and smell its rancid breath on his face and, just when he thought it might pounce on them, the huge dog vanished before his eyes. Turning to his brother, Sam asked if he too had seen the creature vanish but William, staring at his brother blankly, still maintained that he had seen nothing.

Shaken by his experience, Sam decided to stay off work the following day, believing that the phantom dog was a harbinger of some impending doom. He desperately tried to persuade William to do the same, but he was having none of it, and mocked Sam for his superstitious foolery. His pleading was in vain and William went to work down the mine as usual. When the news was carried to Sam that his brother had been killed in a terrible accident at the mine, he was devastated, although not altogether surprised for, in his heart of hearts, he had known that the phantom black dog was an ill omen.

Of recent times there have been many reports in Derbyshire newspapers concerning a phantom black animal that has been seen wandering the countryside. Many newspapers claimed that the animal was a large panther which must have escaped, perhaps some years before, from a private owner who had neglected to inform the authorities for fear that they would be prosecuted. Other individuals investigating the animal claim that it is not even of earthly origins, maintaining that the creature is of alien origin, as the sightings of the black animal tend to also coincide with UFO encounters or sightings. Several people have come face to face with the creature including two teenagers, who ran into the animal in a wood near Duffield, later they described the creature as having huge staring eyes.

The black phantom dogs of folklore are not unique to Derbyshire and the Peak District, indeed they are reported in nearly all parts of the world in almost all doctrines of superstitious belief.

UNIDENTIFIED FLYING OBJECTS (UFOS)

F OR CENTURIES, inhabitants of the hills and valleys of Derbyshire have reported seeing strange luminous lights that flicker and dance around the sky, hills, waterways and wooded areas, often where there are ancient burial mounds or stone circles. These lights were often referred to as Will o'the Wisp, the Jack o'Lantern, Corpse Candle, Foolish Fire or Ignus Fatuus. There have been many attempts by the scientific community to explain these strange moving lights as gas caused by rotting vegetation. Whilst this may explain some of the lights seen, it in no way explains them all, some witnesses to the phen-omena claim that the lights lasted a considerable amount of time, often moving in a meticulous fashion, as if being controlled by an intelligence.

These strange lights were once believed to be spirits, or in some parts of England dragons, which guarded lost treasures, buried priests, kings and places of pagan worship. Turner in *Romances of the Peak* (1901), makes comparisons between Will o'the Wisp and the boggart legend: 'Between Derbyshire and Staffordshire, in the upper part of the Vale of the Dove, there is a piece of marshy land called, locally The Mossco-Carrs. It is rather an eerie place to pass by in the twilight or before the dawn (as) there is a flick-ering light to be seen moving as one moves and it has given rise to many tales of belated travellers having been beguiled by it and led into the swamp, where their bodies remain, and from whence their 'boggarts' arise at night to caper and dance all over the countryside, to the terror of the believing inhabitants.'

Of recent times there has been a great deal of speculation concerning the appearances of UFOs, why they appear, are they of alien origins, military aircraft experiments, or are the mater-ialisations of these strange lights a natural phenomena; so much interest in fact that nearly every county in England is recorded as having a specialist group or society that deal with the subject. Derbyshire's oldest reported incident of strange lights in the sky dates from 1716, when between the hours of 9pm and midnight a bright light appeared in the sky. The parish records of Chapel-en-le-Frith, dated 30 March, record how 'several could have read a book at that time of night... it streamed up like unto long picks, of a large bigness, some black, some the colour of the rainbow, some a whitish colour, and at last it broke into flashes like lightning or smoke, as if it had been smoke of guns, as fast as you could clap your hands, very terrible to behold.'

This description sounds curiously like the Aurora Borealis, or 'Northern Lights'. In the same year it was also recorded that an unusual light was seen in the sky on 6 March. At the time the appearance of the lights caused so much alarm and controversy that a ballad was written entitled *On the Strange and Wonderful Sight that was seen in the Air on the 6th March, 1716*:

The Sixth of March, kind neighbours this is
    true,
A Wonder in the Sky came to my view;
I pray believe it, for I tell no Lye,
There's many more did see it as well as I.

I was on Travel, and was very late,
To speak the truth just about Daylight gate;
My heart did tremble being all alone,
To see such Wonders–the like was never
    known.

These Lights to me like great long spears did
    show,
Sharp at one end, kind neighbours this is true;

I was so troubled I could not count them o'er,
But I suppose there was above a score.

Then I saw like Blood it did appear,
And that was very throng among the spears;
I thought the Sky would have opened in my
    View,
I was so daunted I didn't know what to do.

The next I saw two clouds meet fierce
    together
As if they would have fought one another;
And darkened all these spears excepting one,
They gave a clash an quickly they were gone.

The very last Day in the same month I'm
    told
Many people did strange Sights behold;
At Hartington, the truth I will not spare,

That night they saw Great Wonders in the
    Air.

This Hartington it is in Darbyshire,
And credible persons living there,
They have declared that wonders they did
    view
The very last night in March its certain true.

Today there are still reports of curious objects being seen in the skies of Derbyshire and district. Barely a month passes without some report in a local newspaper of a UFO being seen. One writer has suggested that UFOs are perhaps a type of ghost which we project from our subconsciousness, or that they may be the ghosts of winged creatures which once inhabited the earth but are now extinct, an interesting theory, but one which can never be proved.

THE MERMAID'S POOL

'Her golden hair fell o'er her shoulders white,
And curled in amorous ringlets around her breasts;
Her eyes were melting into love, her lips
Made the very rose envious;
Withal a voice so full, and yet so clear,
So tender, made for loving dialogues.'
Henry Kirke

THERE ARE three pools of water in Derbyshire which are recorded as being the haunt of a mermaid. The first pool is located at Kinder Scout, the second high on the moors between Buxton and Leek, whilst the third is situated near a stoney outcrop known as the Roaches. The first, see (Kinder Scout), is said to be imbued with magical healing qualities if you drink the water at a certain time of year. The second mermaid's pool which lies in remote isolation and known locally as 'Black Mere', has

for centuries been the object of much speculation concerning its ghosts and the depth of the pool, which is said to be bottomless. The third is said to be more sinister.

At Black Mere the mermaid, according to legend, appears on moonlit nights where she sits in the centre, of the pool combing her hair. Another ghost is said to haunt the pool, he is a former victim of the waters who is recorded as having drowned there in the last century. A nearby public house known as the Mermaid Inn, Morridge, records on a plaque inside the building the legend of the mermaid which reads:

> *She calls on you to greet her*
> *combing her dripping crown,*
> *and if you go to greet her,*
> *She ups and pulls you down.*

There is an old story concerning Black Mere which reiterates how a wager was once bet at the nearby Cock Inn, between a party of men and a boastful farmer who, being somewhat inebriated,

The Mermaid's Pool. A mermaid may be seen here at midnight.

After he had managed to calm the victim down, he took her back to the Cock Inn and presenting her like a trophy, then collected his five shillings. The woman, once in the warmth and safety of the inn, reiterated how her attacker was the father of her unborn child who, wanting to conceal her pregnancy, had lured her to the pool where he attempted to murder her. On this occasion the legend of the mermaid had managed to save a life, instead of taking one.

The third Mermaid's Pool, known as the 'Doxy Pool', is located above the rock escarpment known as the Roaches. In 1949, Mrs Florence Pettit, in the company of a friend from Buxton, reported visiting the pool before lunch for a swim where she encountered the mermaid. She later wrote that just as she was about to get into the water: 'A great "thing" rose up from the middle of the lake. It rose very quickly until it was 25 to 30ft tall. Seeming to be part of the slimy weeds and the water, yet it had eyes, and those eyes were extremely malevolent. It pointed its long bony fingers menacingly at me so there was no mistaking its hostility. I stood staring at the undine, water spirit, naiad or whatever it was while my heart raced. Its feet just touched the surface of the water, the weeds and the air. When I dared to look again the creature was dissolving back into the elements from which it had formed.'

bragged that he dared walk across the moors to where the Mermaid's Pool was. The other members of the party soon took him up on his offer and making a collection between them they managed to gather five shillings, a princely sum in those days, which they would give to him when he returned. To prove that he had visited the haunted pool he was to leave his walking stick at the waters' edge.

Setting off from the inn, amidst a storm, the man walked across the moorland pathway which led to the mere. When he was almost at his destination he could hear the cries of a woman. Thinking that it might be the mermaid trying to lure him in, or a trick being played on him by his friends, he hesitated and momentarily considered turning back, when he suddenly heard another pitiful cry. Creeping nearer to the pool he watched in horror as he saw a large framed man attempting to strangle a woman at the waters' edge. Thinking quickly he shouted out loud, as if to some companions, "Come Dick, Jack, Tom, here is the rogue we are wanting!" Whereupon the would-be murderer let go of the woman and fled away in panic.

NINE STONES CLOSE

N HARTLE MOOR, near Birchover, stands Mock Beggar's Hall, named so because it has twin pinnacles, one at each end, which resemble chimneys, giving the rocks the appearance in silhouette of a large house. Also known as Robin Hood's Stride this large outcrop of rocks is believed to have had Druidical associations. Just behind the main rocks there is a small cave within the shadow of an

The carved crucifix at Cratcliffe Hermitage. Close to Nine Stones Close stone circle can be found Cratcliffe Hermitage, the haunt of a monk-type figure.

Nine Stones Close near Birchover. Numerous ghosts haunt the site, which is believed to be one of the most magical places in Derbyshire.

ancient yew tree named Cratcliffe Hermitage, said to be the haunt of garbed figure of a monk. A record of 1549 mentions a payment 'unto ye harmytt for ye brengynge of V Coppull of Counys frome Bradley to Haddon'. At the back of the shelter and carved into the stone is the form of a crucifix, also present is a small niche which probably housed a lamp or candle. The cave is believed to have been used by several hermits over the centuries. These hermits would have helped travellers on the portway since Saxon times. The portway is one of Derbyshire's oldest trackways, parts of which can still be seen today. From a nearby fort the portway descends to Alport, then through Haddon fields and on towards Ashford.

The whole area around Mock Beggar's Hall is abundant in ancient remnants of an almost forgotten age including, burial mounds, an unusual wishing tree, a stone circle and numerous reports of strange lights being seen hovering in the skies.

The stone circle, known as Nine Stones Close, has for centuries aroused much curiosity amongst locals and visitors. The celebrated antiquary Llewellyn Jewitt, together with Canon Greenwell carried out excavations at the site in 1877, but discovered little to throw light on the original purpose of the stones.

Today all that remains of the circle are four stones, although it was recorded in 1829 that there were seven. About 1939 only two of the stones still remained erect. The remaining two that had fallen were re-erected by local archaeologists J.P.Heathcote and his father, J.C. Heathcote. They were assisted by several other workers and the support of the county archaeological society. No one knows what happened to the remaining stones although it is generally presumed that local farmers utilised the stones, perhaps re-cutting them to be used in other areas of the farm.

Writing about the stone circle, in the late 19th

Robin Hood's Stride looking from Nine Stones Close stone circle. Also known as Mock Beggars Hall, this site is believed to be one of the few ancient places, which together with the Nine Stones Close stone circle, curiously aligns with the moon.

century, Derbyshire antiquarian Llewellyn Jewitt said: "Around this Druidical circle it is said – and believed by some of the people of the district – the fairies meet on certain occasions– the full moon, I believe, at midnight and dance and hold 'high jubilee'.

So firmly is this believed that I have been told with extreme seriousness of people who, passing at that time of night, have not only seen the dance but heard the 'fairy pipes' playing for them to dance to. I have heard it seriously affirmed that there were 'hundreds of fairies', gentlemen and ladies, some dancing, others sitting on the stones or on the grass around and others playing the music."

Also in abundance are the local stories concerning strange phantoms and ghostly visitations. I was told by one resident of the area that they had once seen a strange blue light come out of the woods and hover above the stone circle. Other ghosts include a phantom monk, seen near what is known as the 'Hermit's Cave', a white lady, a headless horseman, a green man and the strong belief, according to folklore, that the whole area has a dark history of witchcraft and devil worship.

ROWTER ROCKS

MANY PLACES in Derbyshire have Druidic connections, some places are actually named accordingly like the Druid Inn at Birchover, next to which stands an impressive pile of gritstone towers known as Rowter Rocks. The rocks have long had the reputation of being haunted. The ghost most frequently seen is said to be that of a cloaked figure. Other frightening apparitions are said to appear on moonlit nights, these ghosts wail and weep frighteningly at any lone traveller passing

Rowter Rocks at Birchover. Located behind the Druid Inn at Birchover, Rowter Rocks was once believed to be a sinister place where witches gathered for their Sabbath.

by. Within Rowter Rocks there are alcoves, rooms, carvings and caves. These rocks were once the site of a huge rocking stone, alas this stone is no longer there, a gang of youths toppled it to the ground in the year 1799.

Armchairs have been carved into the rocks and local legend tells that if you were to sit in the middle armchair on All Hallows Eve, when the church clock has just struck midnight, you may hear the wind whispering the name of your true love.

The Reverend Thomas Eyre, who lived at Rowter Hall during the 17th century, was said to have been responsible for the conversion of the rocks to their present state.

According to the legend Thomas Eyre was in fact a dabbler in witchcraft. It is also said that he particularly chose Birchover because the area had a reputation of being a former stronghold of pagan worship.

The Reverend built a church at Rowter, of which very little now remains. This church was believed by some to be an attempt to ease his guilt at having forsaken his Christian teachings. From the top of Rowter Rocks there are beautiful views across the surrounding countryside.

The Druid Inn is also reported to have a ghost, that of an elderly lady who was seen by a customer sitting in the corner of one of the smaller downstairs rooms. According to the lady who saw her, 'One minute she was there the next she was gone'.

The lady concerned distinctly remembers the old lady's smile which she described as 'very warm and caring'.

ROBIN HOOD AND LITTLE JOHN

THE EXPLOITS of Robin Hood are known throughout most of the world. In his life Robin was alleged to have lived at the time of Richard I, Richard the Lionheart, towards the end of the 12th century AD. His base was deep in the forest of Sherwood, namely around the area now occupied by the 'Major Oak', which is purported to have been his principal home. Helped by a band of 'merry men' Robin Hood robbed the rich to give to the poor, and consistently waged war on the notorious and evil Sheriff of Nottingham.

Born at Loxley, Robin is said to have been in line for the title of the Earl of Huntington. His equally famous lady, Maid Marion, who was a Royal Ward, eventually married Robin and helped to obtain a royal pardon for him. Robin was eventually taken into the King's service and later returned to live at Sherwood Forest, where he is said to have finally met his death at the treacherous hands of the prioress of Kirklees in 1247.

Many historians claim that Robin Hood was a myth, a romantic story invented to entertain. Some historians even draw comparisons between the myth of Robin Hood and such alleged historical figures as King Arthur in a bid to dismiss them as mere invented stories. The saga of whether Robin Hood was real or merely a myth will no doubt continue for time to come.

In Derbyshire there are several references to the outlaw. At Hathersage there is a grave which is said to be that of Little John, Robin Hood's right-hand man and faithful companion. The grave, which is situated to the

north-west of the churchyard, sheltered by an ancient yew tree, is now in the care of the Ancient Order of Foresters. In 1784 the grave was opened by Captain James Shuttleworth and was found to contain, amongst other things, a massive thigh bone which measured nearly one metre in length. The thigh bone was removed to a cottage which once stood to the east of Hathersage church nearby, this building no longer exists having been demolished in fairly recent times. The cottage was recorded as being the place in which Little John had ended his years. He had travelled to Hathersage after first placing Robin in his final resting place at Kirklees Park, in West Yorkshire.

After the thigh bone had been taken to the small cottage, which was at that time the home of a Mr Shard, it was measured on a tailor's board. According to one story the huge bone was seen by an old huntsman who remarked that 'No good shall come to either of ye, so long as ye keep dead men's bones above the ground!' Shortly after these words had been spoken James Shuttleworth and his cousin began to experience an array of problems. Finally, remembering what the old man had said, they persuaded the parish clerk to re-bury the bone back in the grave, after which the mysterious misfortunes that had dogged them stopped.

In 1632 it was recorded that at Hathersage Church the hat, bow, arrows and quiver of Little John were kept there. They were eventually removed in 1729, the bow however was taken to

The notorious outlaw, Robin Hood. Could the ghosts of 'green men', at one time referred to as nature spirits and seen across the whole of Britain, be in some way connected to Robin Hood.

The Major Oak at Edwinstowe, Sherwood Forest. Once the home of Robin Hood. It is interesting to note that Robin Hood was synonymously associated with an ancient tree, again reinforcing the belief for some, that Robin and the Green Man of Celtic legend are one and the same.

Cannon Hall near Barnsley; a photo taken of the bow in *c.*1950 shows the weapon to be about 79ins long, (over 6ft), made of spliced yew wood, and would have required a pull of 160lbs to draw it.

In 1847 a Dr Spencer Hall visited Hathersage and sought out Little John's Cottage, which was then occupied by Jenny Shard aged 70 years. Jenny recalled how, as a child of about seven years, she had witnessed the opening of the grave and the huge thigh bone that had been removed. Her father had once told her that the cottage had belonged to Little John and that he had chosen to be buried in the churchyard because he had loved Hathersage village so much.

Some authorities on the supernatural claim that Robin Hood is a parody which has been made between an ancient pagan god of the Forest and woods. It has been suggested that the early

ballads, from which much of the history of Robin Hood has been established, was the first way of recording pagan folklore which before that time had never been written down. This may also account for many places being named after Robin Hood. In Derbyshire we have such place names as Robin Hood's Cave, Robin Hood's Stoop, Robin Hood's Cross, etc. These place names may have nothing to do with the notorious outlaw, instead they may well reflect the belief in the old gods of the Celts who annually acted out the role of walking a man through the forests and woods dressed in green, this was done in a bid to invoke favour from the horned god of nature.

As to the ghosts that haunt Hathersage, there are said to be many. Although it is hard to pinpoint specific stories there are many rumours

The Grave of Little John. A ghost of tall stature seen near to the church entrance is thought to be the spirit of Robin Hood's friend and ally, Little John. A thigh bone was removed from this grave in 1784 which measured nearly a metre in length.

that abound concerning spirits being seen in the district. According to one resident, whom I personally spoke with, there is a ghost that haunts the churchyard. This ghost is apparently over 7ft tall and its ghostly shadow has been experienced on several occasion standing near to the church entrance. It is interesting to note that within this entrance is a medieval stone coffin lid bearing the initials 'J.L.' (John Little), which is thought by many to be the capstone of Little John's original grave.

Throughout Derbyshire, and indeed the whole of the country, there are many other stories concerning the ghosts of 'Green Men', maybe these phantom figures are in some way connected to the legendary story of Robin Hood, or if not him, then perhaps the ancient green man of fertility so fervently worshipped at one time by pagan man?

CHESTERFIELD'S CROOKED SPIRE

ACCORDING to one legend the Devil is accused of having made the twist in the famous spire which has become known internationally. Chesterfield's most famous landmark stretches up 228ft and is thought to have been caused by unseasoned timbers being used. The lead plates on the eight flat sides of the spire are set in herringbone fashion and accentuate the appearance of the twist a lot more than is actually so.

According to one version of the story the Devil is said to have rested on the spire whilst travelling to Derby. As his Satanic Majesty sat there, a service was taking place in the church and as the bride and groom came out of the church the Devil twisted around in sharp surprise to see that the bride was still a virgin.

A similar story tells of the Devil bumping into the spire, having returned from causing much havoc at Nottingham. Flying over the church he was blinded by the goodness of the people attending the service and from that day to this the spire has remained crooked.

THE DERBY RAM

As I was going to Derby,
All on a market day,
I met the finest ram, Sir
That was ever fed on hay,

SO RUNS THE first verse of a very lengthy ballad entitled *The Derby Ram*. Of recent times there has been a great deal of debate as to the origins of this ancient ballad. Some researchers maintain that it has its footings in pagan religious beliefs as the ballad goes on to describe how the animal is slaughtered and how its vast remains are

Chesterfield's Crooked Spire. The Devil is traditionally said to have been the cause of this unusual twist in this famous landmark.

The Derby Ram. Could this ancient symbol be a remnant from our early ancestors who sometimes worshipped sinister gods.

divided and used. The animal has given its name to Derby County Football Club, which is still used as a nickname, as too did the former Sherwood Foresters, Derbyshire's own regiment, who always displayed a magnificent example of the animal as their official lucky mascot.

As to who wrote the ballad it will never be known as the mists of time have swallowed that secret forever. At one time it was thought that the 95th regiment may have been the culprits as they used the ram as their mascot. This idea has been scratched as the earliest account of the ballad being sung is recorded in the 18th century, when of all places the first four verses were reiterated to two young twin boys in Connecticut, America, by no less than George Washington. Since he was of direct English decent it is presumed that he must have picked it up from a member of his family. On this fact alone it has been suggested by some historians that the Derby Ram ballad is far, far, older than first presumed.

Derbyshire's oldest witchcraft coven, known as 'The Order of the Ram', maintain that they have records which can clearly confirm that the Derby Ram is associated with the old Pagan horned God, and which date back several hundred years. In medieval times, and possibly earlier, the Ram along with, the stag, goat and the bull, were all held as the four great phallic symbols. These animals frequently feature in many sacrificial ceremonies and witchcraft legends. For now the mystery of the Derby Ram will remain a secret.

HAUNTED TREES

TREES have appeared to play an important part in many world religions. From the Bo tree, under which the great Buddha sat, to the spectacular Yaggdrasil of Norse mythology, upon which the god Odin hung and spied the runes, through to the barren fig tree which Jesus of Nazareth cursed, and not forgetting of course the Elder tree upon which Judas later hung himself, are all but to name a

Haunted Trees. The author, Wayne Anthony, studying a myriad of tormented and ghostly looking faces in the decaying bark of a haunted tree at the Stoop, Thurvaston.

few, the list appears to be endless. The Druids were said to worship trees and were known as the keepers of the old religion. Their temples were the sacred oak groves, and they believed that all things in creation harboured the spirits of their dead ancestors as well as elemental spirits of nature. The very word Druid is said to translate into 'knowing the oak tree' and the word Der-

went, so common in Derbyshire, means 'abundant in oaks'. The chieftain trees which the Druids worshipped were the oak, apple, rowan, willow, ash, beech and birch. These Celtic beliefs were at one time so widely believed that the Council of Tours in 567 put forth that those who 'worshipped trees, stones, or fountains' should be excommunicated.

Today there is very little left of the ancient groves and mystical woods, which at one time would have been common in Derbyshire, apart from a few random trees which have, at some point in time, been said to be haunted by phantoms, spirits of nature and the little people of folklore and legend.

Derbyshire's most famous tree was undoubtedly a great oak which once resided at the Hagge, a 16th-century building, now a farmhouse west of Staveley at Nether Handley. The tree, known as the Mandrake Tree, or Haunted Oak, was believed to be the only tree in the area that bore Mistletoe. The tree was, for generations venerated by the local people who believed the tree to have healing powers. A macabre feature of the tree was that it was said to bleed thick red blood if ever it was cut and anyone foolish enough to damage the tree were terrified by a blood curdling, half human scream which the tree emitted. The tree eventually blew down in a fearsome storm on the 12th December 1883, believed at that time to be 360 years old.

Another vanished tree, which was said to have the ability to foretell future events, once existed in the grounds of Hassop Hall. The tree, a beech, was believed to whisper the rightful ownership of the Hassop estates, which at one time was under much debate. When the wind blew from the west, stirring the leaves of the tree, it could be clearly heard to whisper 'All hail, true heir, that stills my voice'. Local legend reiterates how several owners of the hall attempted to cut down the tree, but, no sooner had the axe been lifted then the would be destroyer met with some unfortunate accident!

Another ancient tree still living at Darley, this time a yew, is said to be haunted by several ghosts which have been seen periodically over the last century, including the ghost of a pedlar who was murdered a mere 150 yards from the yew. The tree is perhaps one of the oldest yews in England and is thought to be over 2,000 years old, but is more probable to date from Romano-British or Saxon times when the area of the tree could have been a cult centre. A plaque placed near the ancient yew reads: 'There can be little doubt that this grand old tree has given shelter to the early Britons when planning the construction of the dwellings which they erected not many yards to the west of its trunk. To the Romans who built up the funeral pyres for their slain companions just clear of its branches. To the Saxons, converted perchance to the true faith by the preaching of Bishop Diuma beneath its pleasant shade. To the Norman masons carving their quaint sculptures to form the first stone house of prayer, and to the host of Christian worshippers, who from that day to this, have been borne under its hoary limbs in women's arms, to the baptismal font and then on men's shoul-

The ancient Darley Yew Tree. Thought to be over 2,000 years old, this ancient tree is the haunt of several ghosts including a pedlar who was murdered 150 yards from the tree.

ders to their last sleeping place in the soil that gave it birth.'

Near Derby there is a tree known as the witches tree at Shardlow, beneath which the bones of a witch are still said to exist. The tree is surrounded by a gravel pit, which has been excavated around the tree, many local people believe that if the tree is ever removed a curse will be placed on the individual who dares to disturb her bones. Of recent times there has been much debate about the tree, although it is allegedly documented that several centuries ago in a time of religious persecution, individuals were burned at the stake near the spot where the tree grows.

Other trees include the Doveridge Yew, under whose branches Robin Hood and Maid Marion are said to have been married, the ghost of a green man has also been seen near this ancient yew. A votive tree, close to the Nine Ladies stone circle on Stanton Moor, is still used today. Anyone wishing to have a wish come true must tie a strip of their clothing to the tree, repeating their request three times, the wish, I was assured by one practising Pagan lady, is sure to come true.

For those wishing to see spectacular examples of a haunted tree, one need look no further than Wingfield Manor or Long Lane, Thurvaston. Both these trees have an aesthetically haunting charisma. The former is believed to have sprung from a walnut which Anthony Babington dropped whilst sneaking into Wingfield Manor, having first fallen in love with Mary, Queen of Scots, a love which inevitably effectuated both their executions. The latter is a fine example of a revered tree which for centuries was a local convergence point for the community. In times past the now dead oak, which is known to have finally expired in 1929, at The Stoop, Thurvaston, was over the centuries often garlanded on special occasions. The owner, Mr J.Hunt informed me that many strange stories abound about the tree, none of which however, he was prepared to tell, although it is not hard to imagine this once great pendunculate oak; upon which and within the contorted swirls and curves of the rotting bark, one can see all manner of strange and wonderful faces, of what could be interpreted as spirits perhaps still held there. The best face is clearly that of a profile which resembles a bearded man. This unusual face consumes the upper portions of the tree looking curiously like a Druid might look.

SPIRITS OF NATURE

THERE ARE many local legends of people seeing strange creatures, ghosts, goblins, fairies and water spirits in our shire. For generations people have believed that such creatures exist and to disturb, or in any way upset one of them, by cutting a sacred tree down or building a wall across an ancient fairy dell, would inevitably bring about ruin. Farmers were especially wary of nature spirits, and in times past would often plant holly, rowan, or thorn trees near to the farm door, in the belief that the trees, which were themselves believed to have magical powers would protect the house from these mischievous spirits.

Today we may scoff at the idea of a spirit residing in a tree, a cave, a stretch of water or well, but to ancient man residing in the valleys and forests of our region these creatures of antiquity and nature were very real. Many people believe that the green man of legend, Robin Hood, is entirely indigenous to Nottinghamshire when in fact there are reports of him in nearly all the counties in the East Midlands. Some historians, and nearly all those that research the occult and Celtic legend, agree that green men,

A Green Man. These figures, often found carved on churches, are undoubtedly representations of ancient fertility gods, or nature spirits, which were once worshipped by pagan man.

as they have now become known, are most certainly a representation of an ancient fertility god who was also known as The King of May, Jack-in-the-Green, Father of the Wood and Robin of the Hood.

As the people of our country rapidly became Christianised, they adapted their older beliefs into the new doctrine of belief and, not content to entirely let go of the old ways, incorporated many of their mythical figures into the modern fibres of their churches. We need only to look at many of our present day churches that have survived from the 14th, 15th, and 16th centuries to see that the peoples who designed and built them still partly believed in the Celtic gods and spirits.

Many churches still have an abundance of carved stone heads, green men, normally shown with leaves coming out of their mouths, Shiela-na-Gigs (goddess of fertility) seen displaying her genitals, gargoyles, horned men, mouth pullers, dragons and strangely carved animals, all perhaps representations of almost forgotten gods and goddesses.

Our ancestors also knew the value of clean water, it is rumoured that they often sacrificed a young virgin to placate the earth gods and goddesses. Many serious investigators of the paranormal have often pondered why there seems to be so many reported incidents of white ladies haunting the countryside and ancient places. I am reliably informed that it is probably because so many young pure ladies were sacrificed to river gods and bound by druidical magic to protect the place that they gave up their lives for.

Most wells and water stretches seem to be haunted by their own personal ghosts. Many rivers are also said to harbour spirits of nature, and in numerous parts of England it was not uncommon, at certain times of the year, for locals to make special trips to specific stretches of water to drink from them, believing that at strategic points within a year the water was imbued with miraculous healing powers.

These beliefs appear once again to descend from our ancestors who made comparisons with natural phenomena in nature and human anatomy. Certain rivers and water stretches are, at times, known to change colour from yellow ochre, to brown and red, when there has been heavy rain falls and flooding. These superstitious

A Medieval Depiction of a Devil. This ancient painting at Melbourne Church depicts a devil. These creatures were once believed to be spirits of nature which haunted churchyards and woodland groves.

peoples often believed that when the water changed colour it was a sign of a magical transformation, which the spirit of the water, or the gods, were allowing to happen for fertility purposes. So, a river turning red from flooding water running through a clay bed further upriver, was often thought to represent the fact that a god had allowed its own blood to mingle with the waters, thus reinforcing the life giving qualities of the water with the gods own life force. Others believed that the river turning reddish or brown to be an indication of the Earth Mother, or goddess of nature, to be menstruating. While others believed it to be an omen of misfortune and an indication that those once sacrificed to the waters, were reminding all of their presence by the ghostly transformation of the water.

Some people claim that they have visited 'Fairyland', an other-world where there seems to be no human conception of time. One particular story recorded by Derbyshire antiquarian Llewellyn Jewitt in the last century concerns a farm labourer who rested for a short while inside a stone circle and, there found an unusual clay

An Ancient Burial Mound. Burial mounds such as this one in Derbyshire were once believed to be the home of nature spirits, pixies, fairies, goblins, and demons.

pipe, which he cleaned and discovered to be full of a sweet smelling tobacco. So intrigued was he by his find that he lit the pipe and began to smoke it. Very soon a strange sensation began to creep over him, then, all of a sudden he 'found he had the power of seeing what no mortal before had ever seen. In front of him, beneath a large stone, he saw, as it were, the ground transparent and far below, deep down beneath the surface was another world, more beautiful than anything he had ever dreamed of rocks, and trees, and streams, and flowers, and palaces, and beautiful birds were not a tithe of what he saw and more beautiful still, there were hundreds upon hundreds of "small people" gaily dressed, and enjoying and disporting themselves in every imaginable way. It was perfectly fairyland. How long he sat there watching these little folks and admiring the subterranean world of beauties, he did not know but at length the film came back gradually upon his eyes, the smarting returned,

A Shiela-Na-Gig. A pagan representation of a fertility spirit who was said to reside over all the needs of man. Such blatant sexual symbols are often found adapted into many of our Christian churches, a reminder that our forefathers once worshipped more sinister gods and spirits of nature.

the vision passed away, and, his pipe gone out, he was once more able to see as of old.'

Perhaps the clay pipe smoked, with its unusual tobacco mixture, is the pipe and tobacco of ancient legend. Many cultures throughout the world feature very similar stories of earthly substances, normally of fungi origin, having the ability to give man the sight to see spirits, be it of nature or human origins. If the substance was absorbed orally or through the use of ointment or salve, the veil between the two worlds is said to become temporarily lifted, thus enabling man to glimpse other dimensions. The Shamans of North American Indian tribes, with their often wonderful teachings and spiritual philosophies, are known to use a combination of questionable fauna which is often stewed to make a tea, or dried and smoked to induce a trance-like state which enables them to communicate with the spirits of their ancestors. So too do many of the holy men of India, as also do the witch doctors of many African tribes.

HALTER DEVIL CHAPEL

ONE OF THE smallest episcopal chapels in England can be found at Muggington, two miles north-west of Kedleston Hall. The story associated with the church concerns a rather unpleasant farmer, Francis Brown who was given to spending most of his time in an alcoholic stupor. One dark and stormy night, having run out of alcohol, he decided to ride to Derby and buy some more. He sent a young farm worker to fetch his horse from a nearby field, which the boy was unable to do, due to the fact that the thunder and lightning was scaring the horses.

Returning to his master the young farm hand told his master that he could not catch the animal. Francis immediately turned on the boy and, shouted, "I will ride to Derby even if I have to halter the

devil", with that he grabbed the halter and marched out into the night. On arriving outside Francis began to fumble in the darkness until he eventually managed to locate what he thought was a horse. Feeling around he was astonished to find that his horse had sprouted horns. In terror he dropped the saddle and fled. When he recovered from his shock, he vowed to give up alcohol and build a chapel, both of which he eventually did, endowing the chapel with 18 acres of land and stipulating that a service must be held there by the local vicar at least once a month.

Legend has it that the animal Francis Brown tried to halter was in fact a cow. Other versions of the tale tell how the

Halter Devil Chapel at Muggington, where a nefarious farmer once bridled the devil in an attempt to ride to Derby to buy alcohol.

horned animal was no other than the devil, who, hearing Francis' invitation decided to take him up on it. It is said that the chapel was never officially consecrated. Until the end of the 19th century, placed above the door of the chapel, was a curious inscription which read:

'Francis Brown in his old age
"Did build himself a hermitage."

Later someone had added a second verse which read:

'Who being old and full of evil
"He one night haltered the devil."

WIRKSWORTH

THE CHURCH of St Mary was founded in AD652, and houses several examples of fine stone carvings which are believed to have come from an earlier church which stood on the site. One of the country's finest examples of Anglo-Saxon sculpture can be found set into the north wall of the church's interior. The stone coffin lid, with carvings believed to represent the life of Christ, is thought to have once held the remains of an important priest, saint or Mercian King.

The church is undoubtedly built on the site of a much earlier pagan religious site. A stone carved head, now built into the interior of the church's wall, could, according to some authorities, suggest that the area was at one time considered a holy place for Pagans. Such stone heads are believed to have been carved by head worshipping cults. A Celtic ritual of collecting the human heads from slain adversaries was common amongst the ancient peoples who inhabited the valleys and hills of England. Because human heads will

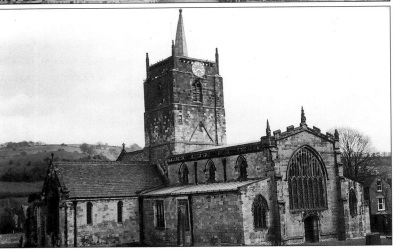

The Church of St Mary at Wirksworth. The custom of 'clypping' which has its roots in paganism, annually takes place at the church on the nearest Sunday to 8th September.

The Wirksworth Stone. This unique stone sarcophagus lid, with carved representations of the life of Christ, is believed to have once held the remains of a famous priest or saint.

eventually perish, it is further believed that religious cults often carved heads in stone as a reminder of who they had slain in battle, this form of preservation may have occurred if the victim happened to be an important rival chieftain or warrior. Other schools of thought suggest that these heads without bodies, were deliberately carved in such a way as to make them easy to transport by Pagans and Celts who were known to be nomadic. A strange custom still prevails at Wirksworth church. On the nearest Sunday to 8th September locals gather at

A carved stone head set into a wall at Wirksworth Church. Were such stone heads once idolised in earlier times by pagan head worshipping cults.

the churchyard to carry out an ancient custom known as clypping. Churchgoers, after having first attended a service at the church, file outside where they place themselves around the church, hold hands and begin to sing 'We love thy place, Oh Lord, in which thine honour dwells'. This ritual is often ended by a procession through the town occasionally attended by the Bishop and other church dignitaries.

This ritual is undoubtedly of pagan origins and is similar to the maypole ritual which is still carried out across England. By embracing the church in such a way it was believed that the individuals would draw from the building, and be imbued with, an essence of holiness. In times passed similar rituals were carried out at sacred groves or around holy trees and rocks. The Wirksworth clypping ritual is undoubtedly a Christianised version of this ancient Pagan practise.

One resident of Wirksworth, whose house overlooks the churchyard, informed me that the graveyard can be an eerie place at night. Once he thought he had seen a skeletal figure in the churchyard and on another occasion he saw a smoky substance rise from the ground, move towards the church and then vanish through the walls.

ASHBOURNE

THERE are several sites in and around Ashbourne that are believed to be haunted. The Wreck, as it is known locally, is a piece of leisure ground which is used by locals as a park. It is here that one might experience the ghost of a 'blue lady' who is seen to wander around the park. A statue that stands within the grounds is also said to be haunted. One local informed me that if one visits the statue at midnight and walks three times around it, the statue will open its eyes, or it might even talk. This is widely reputed within the area to be true and brave young locals, I am informed, regularly go to the site in order to frighten each other.

Hanging Bridge, on the border between Derbyshire and Staffordshire, is the haunt of two spectres. The first is a headless phantom which is to be seen standing on the bridge late at night frightening anyone who dares to pass. The second ghost is a man who is seen to leap off the bridge into the shallow waters below. The bridge is thought to have once been the site of a gallows, hence its name, and is renowned locally as being a place where evil spirits once met.

The magnificent church of St Oswald is home to numerous ghosts. One magnificent tomb, located within the church, is that of Penelope Boothby, who died in 1791 age six years. The tomb which depicts the child in slumber, was created by Thomas Banks, who is perhaps better known for his memorials to Burgess and Westcott in St Paul's Cathedral. The anguish of the parents is movingly expressed in the inscription on the memorial which reads: 'She was in form and intellect most exquisite. The unfortunate parents ventured their all on this frail bark, and the wreck was total'.

The Tomb of Penelope Boothby. Her ghost has been seen wandering about the graveyard on numerous occasions.

Hanging Bridge. Once believed to have housed a gallows, the bridge is the haunt of a headless man and a ghost seen leaping off the bridge.

The churchyard is reputed to be the haunt of three haggard looking ghosts, seen dressed in sackcloth, they are believed to have been victims of the great plague who were laid to rest in the churchyard. Legend tells of many plague victims being buried in this churchyard. Another ghost, this time a child, is seen wandering around the gravestones. It is rumoured locally that the child is no other than Penelope Boothby. She has also been seen standing close to the main gate of the churchyard. One visitor swears that she has seen the ghostly child on several occasions when, as a young girl in the 1920s, she lived in a house which overlooked the graveyard.

REPTON

SAID TO BE the first capital of Mercia, the quiet village of Repton overlooks the River Trent. The village was at one time an extremely important religious centre long before a priory was formed here. The first Christian church of the converted English is thought to have been erected at Repton by four priests who travelled from Northumbria in the 7th century.

The church of St Wystan is believed to have been founded around the time of the Norman conquest, before that the village is thought to have run, not north to south, but east to west, along the banks of the River Trent, rather than down the Repton-Hartshorne valley. As a leading city of Mercia, Repton had an active history which culminated in AD874, when the town and abbey was sacked by the Danes.

Repton has long had an association with

The ancient church of St Wystan at Repton. The haunt of numerous ghosts.

ghostly happenings and strange phenomena. Sir Simon Degge, travelling through Derbyshire in 1727 gives an account of an unusual story which was told to him by a local labourer: 'About 40 years since, cutting hillocks near the surface, he met with an old stone wall. When clearing it further, he found it to be a square enclosure of 15ft. In this he found a stone coffin, and saw in it the skeleton of a human body 9ft long, and round it 100 skeletons of the ordinary size, laid with the feet pointing to the coffin! The head of the great skeleton he gave to Mr Bowes, master of Repton School. I enquired of his son, one of the present masters, concerning it, but it is lost; yet he says, he remembers the skull in his father's closet, and that he often heard his father mention this gigantic corpse, and thinks that the skull was in proportion to a body of that stature. The present owner will not suffer it to be opened, the lady of the manor having forbidden it.'

The huge skeleton was found in a field which is now partly covered by the northern portion of the churchyard. The grave was eventually opened again in the latter half of the 18th century, this dig revealed only a huge assortment of mixed bones. The ghosts and strange phenomena, experienced in the area ever since, appear to suggest that perhaps the disturbance of this grave triggered some malevolent force.

At some time before the mid-19th century the villagers are reported to have gone out with lanterns to search for ghosts. In 1861 three ghosts appeared at two o'clock in the morning and crossing the churchyard they mysteriously vanished. These ghosts were seen by a pupil from the school which overlooks part of the churchyard. One writer a little later suggested that the three ghostly figures may well have vanished into a tunnel which is thought to exist somewhere in the churchyard. The tunnel, according to legend, runs from the churchyard to Anchor Church.

A 17th-century grave digger is also reported to haunt the area around the church. At one time a village grave digger reported being discomforted by the curious figure of a man who would stand watching him, whenever he was digging a grave, from the trees at the edge of the churchyard.

A more sinister spirit, although not seen of recent times, is that of a demonic figure which appeared on numerous occasions bathed in wreaths of smoke sitting upon a gravestone. A similar spirit has been spotted in the crypt of St Wystan. This remarkable crypt, which is believed to have most certainly held the body of St Wystan, is also the haunt of a hooded figure and

a humming ghost which has been heard and seen on three occasions.

Perhaps the most famous ghost at Repton is that of the 'Gallery Ghost' which is known to haunt Repton School. In 1853 Frederick Wickham-Railton, aged 14 years and 8 months, was forced to run the gauntlet. A piece of foolery that many boys were forced to run if their prefect deemed them to have committed an offence.

The Saxon crypt of St Wystan. Phantom humming and the ghost of a monk frequent this eerie crypt.

On the Gallery, which the boys bedrooms opened on to, Frederick was forced to run up and down three times whilst other boys lashed out at him with an assortment of wet towels and pillowcases. One boy, said to have been his brother, tied an ink bottle into the end of his towel and, as Frederick passed, he lashed out at him striking the boy violently on his head, killing him instantly. From that day onward the ghost of Frederick Wickham-Railton came back from the grave to haunt the winner of the annual senior steeplechase. His ghost has also been heard running up and down the gallery late at night.

Repton church is also said to harbour the mischievous spirit of a goblin who is recorded as residing in the 14th-century tower and recessed spire. Only appearing at night, especially if there happens to be a full moon, he will if caught, grant mortals one wish, as long as the wish does not benefit the person who catches it, and that the wish must be made there and then.

Glossary of Ghosts and Terminology

Animal Ghosts

Many experts on the supernatural agree that animal ghosts do exist and believe that the spirits of animals also survive the death process. There are many books which specifically deal with the issue of animal ghosts, perhaps the most recognised one being written by ghost hunter Elliot O'Donnell, who says in his book *Animal Ghosts* (1913): 'The mere fact that there are manifestations of "dead" people proves some kind of life after death for human beings; and happily the same proof is available with regard for a future life for animal; indeed there are as many animal phantoms as human — perhaps more.'

There is also a school of thought which believes that animals have what is known as a 'collective soul'. This suggests that five, or even more animals at one time, may share one soul. This may be hard to believe, but the theosophical implications of what a shared soul could possibly mean are indeed enormous.

Apparition

An apparition is said to be the ghost of someone the person seeing it knows, or a ghost which appears in human shape, looking and appearing as if it were alive but was in fact long dead.

The tradition of apparitions goes back to the earliest of times and documented accounts are numerous in the pages of history. Some apparitions are known to appear only when some disaster is about to happen, whilst there are those which are known to guard sacred places. Apparitions are not always visual, they are often heard or felt.

Banshee

The banshee, or 'bean si', as this spirit should be correctly pronounced, is undoubtedly Ireland's most famous ghost. Said to follow ancient Irish families, she is more likely to be seen by a third daughter and is more commonly said to follow a family if the first letter of their surname is 'O'.

She is said to appear prior to the death of a family member and announces the death by crying and wailing during the night hours. The sound which she emits, is said to be like that of two cats fighting only much worse. She is known to cry about the death of a relative who is thousands of miles away in another country, and is reported to appear several nights in succession until the actual death occurs. She is often described as being small, appearing either as a horrible hag dressed in rags who sometimes emits a strange smell, or as a young and beautiful woman dressed in a green dress. The eyes are always said to be red and swollen from constant crying. There is a third type, but no one knows whether she is young or old, as she has no clear features, often being described as having holes where her eyes and nose should be. All three types are described as having very long hair which streams out in the wind. If the banshee is disturbed by a moral she will not appear again whilst that generation lives, but will return to haunt future generations.

Boggart

The name boggart is a word mainly used in the North of England and is used to describe a particularly nasty type of ghost. Boggarts are said to have a habit of crawling into people's bedrooms at night and pulling the bedclothes off, pinching, slapping and biting, especially feet. Those unlucky enough to see one will get a shock, for they are said to be fearsome looking with sharp, bright, long and yellowing teeth.

Bogie

The bogie is a rather unpleasant spirit and especially favours haunting children hence, 'If you don't stop being naughty the bogie man will get you!' According to British folklore, bogies are black in appearance, have ugly grinning faces and are short and hairy with a foul smell about them. They were once thought to be the most powerful amongst ghosts for they had once served the Devil by doing evil deeds against mankind. They have been known to make wailing noises, in the wind, similar to the Irish banshee.

Birds

There are many instances of birds returning as ghosts. Birds were at one time believed to be messengers of the dead and when a bird often tapped on a window it was looked upon as meaning that a ghost was looking for another spirit to join it. Certain birds, sparrows, larks and storks, were said to carry the souls of people from the Guff (Hall of Souls) in Heaven, to earth. Other birds, more especially crows, were believed to carry the spirits of humans on to the next plain of existence.

Cats

Said to be the most common form of animal haunting next to dogs. The ghost cat is believed to have its spooky origin in ancient Egypt where cats were often worshipped especially at Bubastis, where many thousands of mummified cats have been excavated.

Historically the Devil was believed to be able to take the form of a cat. Elliot O'Donnell in his *Occult Review* (1962), reports: 'There are, at the present moment, many houses in England haunted by phantoms in the form of black cats, of so sinister and hostile in appearance, that one can only assume that unless they are actual spirits of cats, earthbound by cruel and vicious propensities, they must be vice elementals, *ie* spirits that have never inhabited any material body, and which have either been generated by vicious thoughts, or else have been attracted elsewhere to a spot by some crime or vicious act once perpetrated there'.

Clairaudiant

The ability to hear disembodied voices of the dead, or other entities, who normally tell of events yet to happen. Many mediums claim the ability to hear dead relatives and pass on information from a place they call the 'Spirit World'.

Clairsentient

An ability to be able to feel things in a divinitory sense. To know things in a divinitory sense. To know this which have been, are, and are yet to be. Those who claim to have this ability state that it is basic human instinct finely attuned and polished.

Clairvoyant

The ability claimed by some to be able to see visions of events yet to happen, happening, or that have happened. This word in its simplest form basically means 'to see with sight beyond the normal human range of sight'.

Crossroad Ghosts

Crossroads have long been associated with hauntings, and although it is not clear as to exactly why, some interesting theories are still to be found. Ghost hunter Elliot O'Donnell in this book *Haunted Britain* (1948) suggests the following: 'Some think it is because in olden times, murderers, sorcerers and suicides were buried at crossroads, with a stake thrust through them in a foolishly vain attempt to keep their spirits from wandering; others think it is because witches and wizards were believed to hold orgies and practise the Black Art at crossroads while others, again, think crossroads, like lonely pools, old quarries and some woods, have a peculiar attraction for a certain species of spirits.'

Other researchers maintain that crossroads are more likely to be haunted because of the amount of suicides which were buried there. The superstition of interring the dead at such places lies in the Christian belief of the cross being a form of protection from demons, vampires and such supernatural night creatures. This, however, is thrown into doubt when we consider that excavated human remains near crossroads and predating Christianity have been unearthed all over the world.

Deathwatch

This strange turn of phrase is connected to a species of beetle known as the deathwatch beetle which taps on wood. It was believed by many that the beetle could sense the presence of death and tapped in acknowledgement of spirits arriving to take the soul to its next destination.

Dogs

Ghost dogs are reported all over the British Isles and are said to vary in size. They can be small with extremely large eyes, be white, black, vicious or of a gentle disposition. In Lancashire they have a ghost dog known as a Striker, in Wales there is the Gwyllgi, whilst here in Derbyshire we have the Rach Hounds and Gabriel's Ghost Hounds which are often heard in or near Chesterfield.

Doppelganger

The word is derived from German and is an expression for a ghost which is actually the double of a living person. Those who experience seeing their double are said to be heading towards misfortune in the near future. Some writers maintain that the doppelganger can also be an indication of good fortune, although recorded incidents of them being good omens are rare. They are alleged to be in every way like the person that they are haunting, being as their twin. Other people associated with the haunted individual are also reported as having seen the doppelganger at a place where the living counterpart was nowhere near.

Drude

The drude is an ancient English expression for a nightmare ghost which a mature witch or wizard, well versed in the art of magic, who is said to be able to inflict a ghost into the dreams and nightmares of their chosen victim.

Duppy

The duppy is a well-known West Indian ghost which can be summoned from its grave to do the bidding of a witch by certain ceremonial magic which involves mixing blood and rum, together with several other substances. This is then thrown on to the grave of one known to have been an evil person when alive, as the duppy is believed by many to be the personification of evil in a human. The duppy is said to be only able to walk the earth between the hours of dusk to cock-crow.

Ectoplasm

This strange substance is said to be extruded from the sweat glands, mouth, nostrils and genitals of certain mediums whilst in a trance-like state.

The word ectoplasm, or teleplasm, as it is now frequently referred to as being, is derived from the Greek words ektos and plasma, meaning exteriorised substance. Some researchers claim that the substance is not unlike pale white tissue paper, cheesecloth, fine silk strands which all gather together to make a human shape. Other schools of thought insist that the substance is like human and animal tissue and several investigators claimed to have examined the substance stating that its biological chemistry is, at present, unknown to man.

Elementals

These strange ghosts are said to be spirits which have never existed in human form, unlike normal ghosts and spirits which have at one time, been and lived as a human. Occultists declare them as being ancient spirits, which predate man, which fall into four categories consisting of earth, air, fire and water. Elemental spirits are often associated with haunted stretches of woodland and rivers, mountains and valleys.

Elves

These spirits of nature are believed to be spiteful creatures and were said to be lost souls trapped between the two worlds, not evil enough to go to Hell, but not quite good enough to be accepted into Heaven.

Exorcism

An exorcism is an act of religious ceremony which expels a spirit which may have taken up residence in a house or human being. The ceremony normally consists of a priest or clergyman, who is often specially trained, and who will say prayers and repeat loud exhortations, often burning candles and sprinkling holy water whilst incense is burnt. This ritual is a modern version of the old Christian rite of excommunication, which was known as the rite of 'Bell, Book and Candle', where sinners were eliminated from further entering the faith by a priest who would ring a small bell and slam the *Holy Bible* shut, often after reading the Maledication, and extinguish the burning candles.

Modern mediums also claim to be able to perform such an act, normally without the trappings, by psychically contacting the spirit which may be causing the trouble and convincing it to move on to the next spiritual plane of existence. Many mediums believe that ghosts are spirits who have not come to terms with their passing, which may often have been untimely and tragic, or that in some way they are being held back from progression on a spiritual level by someone or, more often than not, something in this world.

Extras

This widely used term is now regularly used to describe faces, or whole images of people, who mysteriously appear on photographs. There are many instances of pictures being developed to reveal a long-dead relative, or occasionally someone who may be alive but thousands of miles away. Often the pictures show white wispy cloudlike substances out of which a face is normally starting to appear. In the early days of spirit photography (a claim to be able to photograph the dead), many alleged spirit faces were deliberately introduced into the photographs, which unfortunately have nearly all been proved to be fraudulent.

There are, however, a small number of photographs which defy explanation, many showing people or faces of the dead, and these pictures are believed to be genuine. One such picture was taken of a lady in blue at St Werburgh's Church, Spondon by a Miss Gwen Nicholls, who was casually taking photographs of the interior of the church in the mid-1970s. The strand phenomena of extras are discussed at length in Harry Price's fascinating book, *Search For The Truth: My Life Of Psychical Research* (1942).

Fairies

Fairies are said to be small, often tiny, invisible creatures. They can be of great help to those they favour or of great hindrance to those who upset them. The colour green is sacred to them and their place of abode is in the hills, valleys, amongst the trees, where there are ancient burial mounds and mysterious stone circles.

Fire Ball

Frequently reported and most commonly said to be seen in Scotland. The fire ball is said to be a medium to large sphere which moves in a smooth and often slow way, more frequently reported near large stretches of water, although this is not always the case as in the fire ball which has been seen on the Arboretum and also those at Derby River Gardens. They are believed to be the souls of the departed returning to earth to guide the souls of the recently departed to the next world.

Galley Beggar

This is believed to be an old English ghost which is often reported in the North of England and is mentioned as far back as 1584, in Reginald Scot's work, *The Discovery of Witchcraft*. The ghost is said to be like a skeleton or is often described as barely having any flesh upon it. The name is derived from the word 'gallery', meaning to frighten or terrify. This ghost may be often encountered on country roads frequently with the head tucked beneath its arm whilst emitting a terrifying scream.

Ghoul

The ghoul was at one time the common word for a ghost in Arabia. These days, however, the word is commonly used throughout the world to define a particularly nasty or often vicious looking ghost. In the Eastern world the ghoul was believed to be a spirit which looks almost human, having a terrifying face. The ghoul was believed to gain sustenance from eating human flesh, especially the flesh of corpses, hence the word ghoul is often used to describe ghosts which specifically haunt graveyards.

Graveyard Ghost

According to folklore, the first person to be buried in a churchyard was believed to return as a ghost to guard the site against the Devil. This ghost was believed to have special abilities. Because the task was so great, a black cat or dog was often buried before any human so as it would become the guardian of the dead and remain so until the Crack of Doom.

Gremlin

Gremlins have only appeared in recent times and although the word is now widely used, it actually originated from World War Two when pilots flying dangerous missions reported seeing strange goblin-like creatures in the aircraft with them. Alasdair Alpin MacGregor in his book, *The Ghost Book* (1955), wrote: 'Members of the Royal Air Force, who participated in the Battle of Britain, have told me of them and, although the *Oxford English Dictionary* fails to include the word, a professor at Oxford tells his friend, the eminent A.L.Rowse, that the gremlins 'have been at me all my life'. Gremlins certainly are here to stay as Steven Spielberg immortalised them in his highly-acclamied films of these supernatural creatures, and now it seems not a piece of machinery can naturally go wrong without someone saying, 'there's a gremlin in the works'.

Grey Ladies

Said to originate from Tudor times when the Dissolution of the Monasteries resulted in the death of many monks and nuns who would have then been habited in grey. Many investigators of hauntings and ghosts claim that the theory of grey lady ghosts is similar to that of the white ladies.

Other investigators claim that the colour which a ghost appears is relevant to surrounding substances, wood, plaster, stone, shrubbery etc., which may be contributing to the ghosts appearance.

Halloween

Originating long before the advent of Christianity, the 'Feast Of The Dead', perhaps being a better name for the night, was a tune of great celebrations for our ancient pagan ancestors, who would light great bonfires across the country to summon the dead and placate them by offering burnt sacrifices, and warmth from the fires to help the ancient dead through the cold winter months.

The Christian Church moved the bonfire tradition to 5 November to mark Guy Fawkes' fate in hope of masking the true meaning of the night. To this day modern witches still celebrate the night on 31 October by holding feasts and performing magic rituals. According to legend, on the stroke of midnight the gates of Hell were opened by Satan himself and all the spirits of evil were set free on earth to wreak havoc. By cock crow all evil spirits must return to Hell whose gates were shut tight at the first sight of dawn, any spirits left outside would thus be disintegrated forever.

Haunted Chairs

There are many reported instances throughout England of owners who had a particular fondness for or who may have died in an armchair, coming back as a ghost and being seen in that particular chair. In Derby there is a haunted chair at the Greyhound public house in Friar Gate. It is said that if you are male, have a certain name and are a certain age, then you should not sit there. Apparently, four men unfortunate enough to share these characteristics did and shortly afterwards each one died.

Haunting

This word is used to describe a ghost which is seen on more than one occasion within the same building or at the same place. Therefore, when a ghost, or ghosts, are seen at the same place on successive occasions, we refer to the place as being haunted. People can also be haunted as can any item which may have belonged to someone deceased.

Headless Ghosts

These ghosts are believed to be the spirits of people who had died by being beheaded, although there is a wealth evidence to suggest that these types of apparitions may be connected to a far more ancient practice of beheading corpses, especially when they were in any way believed to be connected to witchcraft or sorcery. Graves found at Little Chester revealed several such burials with decapitated heads being placed between the knees, perhaps in the feeble

hope that the dead would not come back to haunt the living.

Iron

Believed by many to be a sure antidote against all kinds of bad magic and evil spirits who, it is claimed, hated the very sight of the substance.

Headless Horsemen

The headless horsemen of ghost tradition is said to be a result of a rider who may have been ambushed and decapitated whilst riding swiftly though a wooded glade, as it is in such places that one might encounter such a spectral creature. Other theories state that the headless riders are ancient chieftains who lost their heads in battle and still wander the face of the earth seeking to find their dismembered heads. One other theory concerning headless horsemen and coach drivers is that they may have lost their heads whilst passing through coaching archways.

Lemures

Lemures is the name given to evil ghosts by the Romans, who believed that spirits of the dead often returned to haunt relatives and friends. Said to be especially active during certain months of the year, certain ceremonies to placate these spirits were often held in ancient Rome. Several elaborate funeral ceremonies could be presented to the gods to ensure that the return of the dead person's spirit would not happen.

Materialisation

The ability claimed by certain mediums to be able to bring into visible sight a spirit of ghost. One of the first recorded incidents of materialisation occurred in America in 1860, by the Fox Sisters, founders of modern day spiritualism.

Mermaid Pools

Also known as pools of doom, death pools, or back water, these often secluded ponds and lakes, are said to be haunted by a certain type of mischievous ghost. Many people claim that these places emit an uncomfortable feeling of sadness and melancholy. Most of these pools have, at some time or another, been reputed to have had individuals drown there.

Ouija Board

Consisting of 38 pieces of card, normally arranged around a table, each card has a different letter of the alphabet written upon it, whilst upon nine others are written the numbers zero to nine and upon two other cards the words 'yes' and 'no'. The Ouija, or Wee Gee board, as it is now so often called, is alleged to be a mediator between the world of the living and that of the dead. When all the necessary arrangements are made, and the required amount of people are present, a glass beaker or wine glass is placed on the table and the consultation with the board can begin.

Perfumed Ghosts

Some investigators in the paranormal maintain that a ghost can manifest itself in the form of a scent. Many people have experienced smelling a perfume which may have been a favourite scent of a deceased relative, such as an aunt or grandmother. Other smells are said to be horrible such as fish, faeces, burning etc. The most famous local case is one which happened in Derbyshire and was recounted in a letter sent by a Dr James Clegg in 1745, to a colleague, the Revd Dr Ebenezer Latham: 'I know you are pleased with anything curious or uncommon in Nature, and if what follows shall appear such I can assure you from eye witnesses of the truth of every particular. In a church at about three miles distance from us, the indecent custom still prevails of burying the dead in a place set apart for the devotions of the living yet the parish not being very populous, one would scarce imagine the inhabitants of the grave could be strai'tned for

want of room yet it should seem so, for on the last of August, several hundreds of bodies roase out of the grave in the open day in that church, to the great astonishment and fear of several spectators.

'They deserted the coffin, and arising out of the grave, immediately ascended directly towards heaven, singing in concert all along as they mounted thro' the air; they had no winding sheets about them, yet did not appear quite naked, their vesture seem'd streaked with gold, interlanced with sable, skirted with white, yet thought to be exceeding light by the agility of their motions, and the swiftness of their ascent.

'They left a most fragrant and delicious odour behind them, but were quickly out of sight, and what is become of them or in what distant regions of this vast system they have since fixed their residence, no mortal can tell.

'The church is in Hayfield, three miles from Chappell Frith. 1745.'

Phantom Coaches

Also known as death's messenger, the phantom coach is believed by many to be seen prior to a death in the family of the person seeing it. The coaches are said to always be black and can be either a genuine coach or a hearse, the horses are always said to be headless, and the driver, when his features are clear, is more often than not said to be skeletal, or hideously ugly, with a fixed grin. The coach as it passes, which is sometimes at great speed, is said to be always silent and if anyone happens to accidentally get in the way of the coach and horses they will be carried away to their doom.

Poltergeist

The word poltergeist is derived from the German verb polter, meaning to create noise by banging, knocking or throwing things about, and the noun geist, meaning ghost. Harry Price, one of the greatest authorities on ghosts, describes beautifully the antics, and make up, of this complex and nearly always unwanted spirit in *Poltergeist Over England* (1945): 'A Poltergeist is an alleged ghost, elemental, entity, agency, secondary personality, 'intelligence', 'power', 'spirit', 'imp' or 'familiar' with certain unpleasant characteristics, whereas the ordinary ghost of our storybooks is a quiet, inoffensive, timed, noiseless, and rather benevolent spirit, with usually friendly feelings towards the incarnate occupants of any place where it has its abode, the Poltergeist is just the reverse. According to the many reports of its activities, in all lands and in all ages, the Poltergeist is mischievous, destructive, noisy, cruel, erratic, thievish, demonstrative, purposeless, cunning, unhelpful, malicious, audacious, teasing, ill disposed, spiteful, ruthless, resourceful, and vampiric. A ghost haunts, a Poltergeist infests. A ghost likes solitude, a Poltergeist prefers company. A ghost seeks the half-light a Poltergeist will "Perform" in sunlight'.

Psychic

Pertaining to the soul and mind, being a mystic, clairvoyant, telepathic etc., or having a combination of supernatural abilities which allows the individual to perceive time differently. The ability to see or sense the future, present and past. Not to be confused with the word 'spiritual' which is so often used these days to describe mediums who do not need to be psychic to be spiritual but do need to be spiritual in order to be psychic.

Psychomancy

The ancient art of reading future events by the appearance of ghosts, and spirits, and what their manifestations to the living might mean.

Salt

Believed, in ancient customs of the dead and sacred myth to be a universal antidote against all manner of witchcraft and evil spirits. Anyone carrying salt in their pockets are said to be protected, even the Devil himself would not approach anyone carrying the substance. Salt is also said to subdue wicked spirits haunting a dwelling if it is placed in each and every corner of the rooms within the building.

Seance

A seance normally involves a medium who claims to be able to contact deceased relatives, or occasionally spirit guides, and even strangers, by means of materialisation of a spirit or disembodied voices. Knocking and rapping sounds may also be apparent during a seance. The word seances is French in origin meaning a sitting and there is no absolute limit as to how many people can be present, although it is generally accepted that the even numbers seem to have better results.

Spectre

Once used as another word to describe a ghost but now the word is most commonly used to describe a ghost which has been found to be faked or is explained away by natural occurrences.

Talisman

An object, charm, mascot, amulet, which can be worn, kept close to oneself, or more often than not placed near, or buried close to the home. These objects are said to have the ability to ward off evil and keep ghosts at bay.

Telepathic

The ability to read minds and know the thoughts of other people, either near, or as is often reported, at a great distance.

Trance

The ability to lower the state of consciousness, between sleeping and wakefulness, where the medium claims to be able to use their bodies as a channel for waiting spirits to use and pass information through to living relatives and friends.

Vengeful Spirits

There are many instances of ghosts returning from the dead to avenge themselves of terrible wrongs which have been done to them. The most famous local avenging spirits are those of Alan and Clara, who were brutally murdered, by five miners at the Winnats Pass (windy gates) near Castleton, Derbyshire, see (Winnats Pass).

Wakes

This ancient custom, almost unique to Ireland, of sitting and watching over the dead whilst vast amounts of alcohol are consumed, is a tradition in which it is believed that by consuming the alcohol it will help the spirit of the deceased on its journey to the spirit world. The use of alcohol is partly in the belief that it will help cleanse the sins of the deceased. The reasoning behind a wake lies in the ancient belief that an evil spirit may try to sneak into the body before the soul has had a chance to try its luck at Heaven's gates. Noise is created at a wake by music, sing and laughing, in the Celtic belief that such loud noises will keep evil spirits away.

Warlock

Used by many writers to describe a male witch. Many male witches, however, would find this title insulting as the word has been used in times past to describe a traitor.

White Ladies

White Ladies are seen all over the British Isles, and the Peak District has its fair share of them. They traditionally haunt castles, mansions, halls and, unusually, bridges or stretches of water. The reason for white ladies being seen near water, according to one writer from France, is that in ancient times pagans were said to sacrifice young ladies to river gods, thus supposedly allowing them safe passage across.

Will 'o the Wisp

Also known as jack-o-lantern, ignis fatuus, corpse candle, foolish fire, etc. There are many reports of this phenomenon in the Peak District, Stanton Moor, the Weaver Hills, Monsal Dale, and any- where near marshland. Traditionally these spirits were believed to guard lost treasures, buried priests, kings and places of pagan religious worship. Those foolish enough to follow these strange dancing lights were inevitably led to their deaths in marshland bogs. Legend has it that the lights were souls of dead murderers and evil people, cursed to wander the face of the earth forever, seeking to find peace until the end of the world.

Witch

A person, especially a woman who practises witchcraft. There are many different types of witches. Most worship nature and call upon gods and goddesses of fertility to help them in their magical undertakings. One interesting unwritten law concerning witches, is that they are for- bidden from telling anyone what they are, or how they practise their art, believing that silence is power and power brings knowledge. Most modern witches would not use their abilities to harm anyone, instead choosing to help and pro- mote human, animal and spiritual awareness of a greater wisdom of life than what is obviously apparent. A witch uses 'bad magic' on only rare occasions, as another unwritten law states that evil can only be justified if used for the greater good of the whole, making it difficult for the witch to decide how they will act when there may be a need to use bad magic.

Wizard

A person with amazing abilities, one normally well versed in the art of magic. Most male witches prefer this title.

GLOSSARY

Wraiths

According to old traditions, a wraith is the ghost of a person on the verge of death and often appears as an exact likeness of their human counterpart. They are regarded as a death omen and should a person see a wraith of themselves, then their days are numbered.

The most famous instance of an individual seeing a wraith was the poet Percy Bysshe Shelley, (1792-1822), who saw his own wraith as he stepped on to a small boat which was to take him across the Bay of Spezzia in Italy. Shelley had arranged to meet with his friend, Leigh Hunt, and was eager to see him again. Needless to say, the boat foundered in the storm, Shelley was drowned and the omen of the wraith was fulfilled.

Bibliography

Edited by W.Andrews, *Bygone Derbyshire.* (1892)

Barnatt, John, *Stone Circles of the Peak.* (Turnstone Books, 1978)

Bord, Janet and Colin, *The Secret Country.* (Book Club Associates 1976)

Daniel, Clarence, *Ghosts of Derbyshire.* (Dalesman, 1973)

Daniel, Clarence, *Haunted Derbyshire.* (Dalesman, 1975)

Daniel, Clarence, *Derbyshire Traditions.* (Dalesman, 1975)

Daniel, Clarence, *The Story of Eyam Plague.* (Bakewell & Wye Valley Press 1983)

Elder, Isabel Hill, *Celt, Druid and Culdee.* (Covenant Publishing Co. Ltd. 1962)

Graham J.McEwan, *Haunted Churches of England.* (1989)

Green, Andrew, *Phantom Ladies.* (1977)

Hippisley-Coxe, Anthony D., *Haunted Britain.* (Hutchinson & Co, Ltd. 1973)

Jewitt, Llewellyn, *Derbyshire Ballads.* (London 1867)

Litchfield R.M., *Strange Tales of the Peak.* (J.Hall & Sons 1992)

McGregor, A.A., *The Ghost Book.* (Robert Hale, 1955)

Merrill, John, *Derbyshire Folklore.* (J.N.M. 1988)

Mitchell, W.R., *The Haunts of Robin Hood.* (1970)

Naylor, Peter J., *Celtic Derbyshire.* (Hall, Derby 1983)

Naylor, Peter J., *Manors and Families of Derbyshire, Vol, 1&2.* (Hall, Derby 1984)

Pickford, Doug, *Magic, Myth and Memories.* (Sigma Leisure 1993)

Power, E.G., *Hanged for a Sheep.* (Scarthin Books 1981)

Rhodes, Ebenezer, *Peak Scenery.* (1824)

Rickman, R. and Nown G., *Mysterious Derbyshire.* (Dalesman, 1977)

Rogers, Frank, *Curiosities of the Peak District.* (Moorland 1979)

Taylor, Phillip *May the Lord Have Mercy on Your Soul.* (Hall, Derby 1989)

Toulson, Shirley *Exploring the Ancient Tracks and Mysteries of Mercia.* (1980)

Turner, W.M. *Romances of the Peak.* (London 1901)

Underwood, Peter *The Ghost Hunters Guide.* (Blandford Press 1986)

The Peak District Companion. (David and Charles 1981)